SCIENCE-*OLOGY*

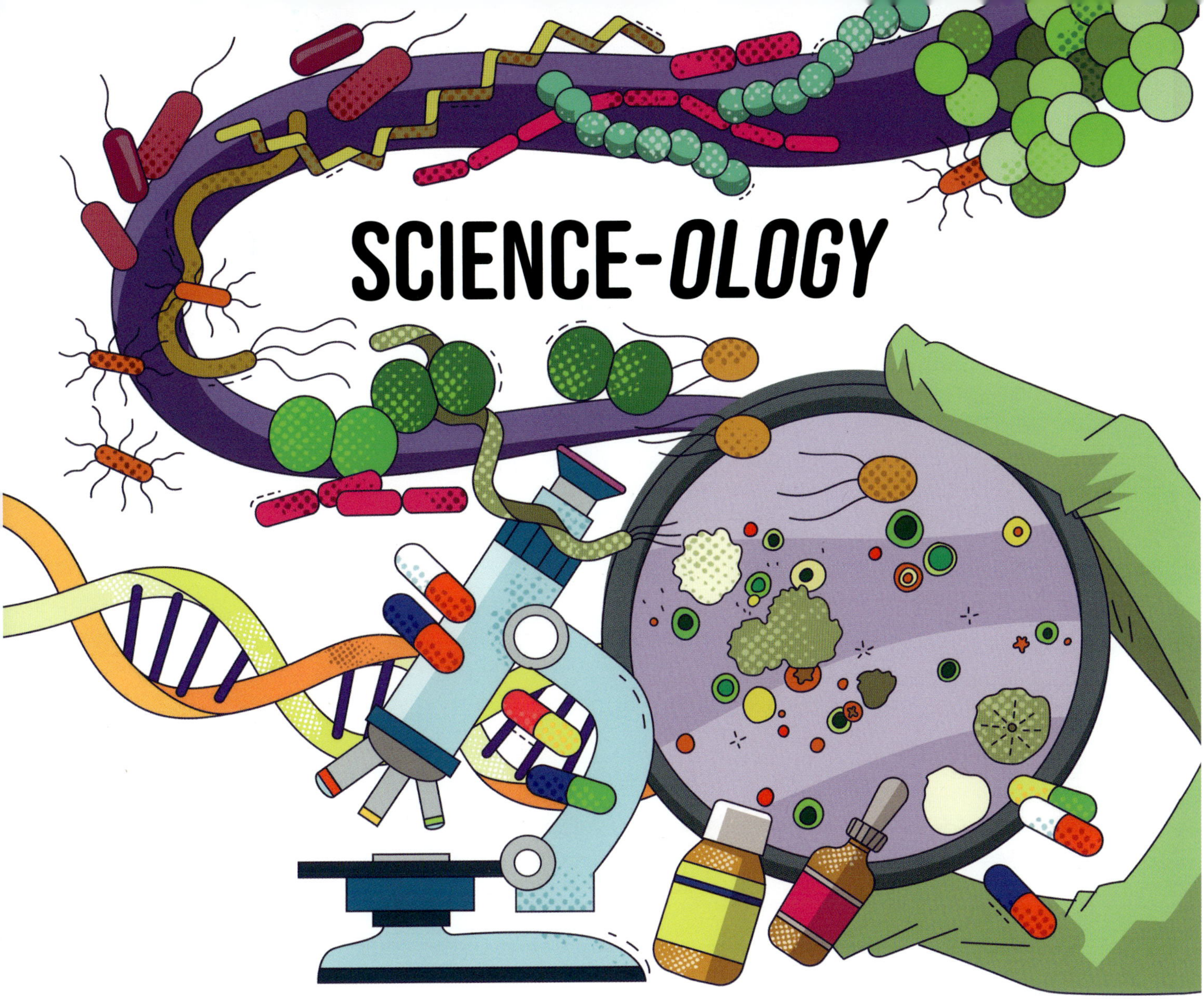

BACTERIOLOGY

ANNA CLAYBOURNE
DANIEL LIMÓN

PowerKiDS press

Published in 2026 by The Rosen Publishing Group, Inc.
2544 Clinton Street, Buffalo, NY 14224

First published in Great Britain in 2023 by Wayland

Editor: Elise Short

Consultant: Nathan North, Operational Lead, Microbiology Royal London Hospital, NHS East and South East London Pathology Partnership

Design: Rocket Design (East Anglia) Ltd

Illustrations: Daniel Limón

Cataloging-in-Publication Data

Names: Claybourne, Anna, author. | Limón, Daniel Sanchez, illustrator.

Title: Bacteriology / by Anna Claybourne, illustrated by Daniel Limón.

Description: Buffalo, NY : PowerKids Press, 2026. | Series: Science-ology | Includes glossary and index.

Identifiers: ISBN 9781499454666 (pbk.) | ISBN 9781499454673 (library bound) | ISBN 9781499454680 (ebook)

Subjects: LCSH: Bacteria--Juvenile literature.

Classification: LCC QR74.8 C539 2026 | DDC 579.3--dc23

Picture credits: Alamy: Science History Images 27cl; Science Photo Library 43bl; The History Collection 10bl.

Getty Images: Steve Northrup 40t.

NASA: 42b.

Kent Nishimura: 39bl.

Science Photo Library: Dennis Kunkel Microscopy 39br; Moredun Animal Health Ltd 20tl; Dr Linda Stannard, UCT 11cr; Volker Steger 41t.

Shutterstock: Abscent Vector 27cr; Arc Tina 29rc; Arcady 10br; Rauf Aliyev 29crc; Angellodeco 13tc; Art Studio G 19cr; Peddalanka Ramesh Babu 4tr; Barks 19t; Elif Bayraktar 33tl; Berkut 29clc; Borzywoj 35b; Briddy 4t, 33bg; Choksawatdikorn 33cl; r.classen 22c; Sirikwan Dokuta 12b; Everett Collection 22t; Maple Ferryman 14cl; Flash Vector 5b; Fotovpl 8bcr; Dacian Galea 6b; Girlwander1982 33bl; GoodStudio 45b;Gorodonkoff 45t; Pavel Hlystov 25b; Passagorn Hosakul 15cl; Incomible 41bc; Irabel18 5c; Egudin Ka 41br; Kichigin 33c; H-Ko 12t; Axel Kock 30t; Kateryna Kon 9t, 9bl, 9br, 16tr, 20tr, 20b, 34; Akong Kong 26c; KPixMining 8c; light_s 29c; Macrovector 5cl; Larina Marina 43br; Martial Red 19c; Filip Milovanovic 33tr; M-O Vector 4c; mything 27b; Neonic Flower 41bcl; 9foto 5cr; Pattikky 13c; Photoroyalty 22b; supanut piyakanont 29cl; Arpon Pongkasetkam 12c; Qualit Design 5tr; Rasulov 22ct; Rob J808 38t; Sakmeniko 7t; Schira 13bl; SciPro 8bl; Tatiana Shepeleva 8bc; Slowmotiongli 33cr; Serhiy Smirnov 29cr; Stefano73 18-19; Strejman 29lc; Stockphoto mania 25c; Sukjai Photo 13tr; Svtdesign 41bl; Sww 32t; Anatta_Tan 35t; Tarpan 33tc; 3DDock 19tc; Peter Titmuss 19b; Pete Turner Photography 5tl; Uncle Leo 17c; Urfin 20br; Vector street 19tr; Vega 7 44b; Yakobchuk Viacheslave 4b; Youlanda Yhola 23t.

Wikimedia Commons: H Lenthall 23br; Wellcome Collection 23bl, Ernest Board 7b; US National Library of Medicine.

Manufactured in the United States of America

CPSIA Compliance Information: Batch #CSPK26. For further information contact Rosen Publishing at 1-800-237-9932.

CONTENTS

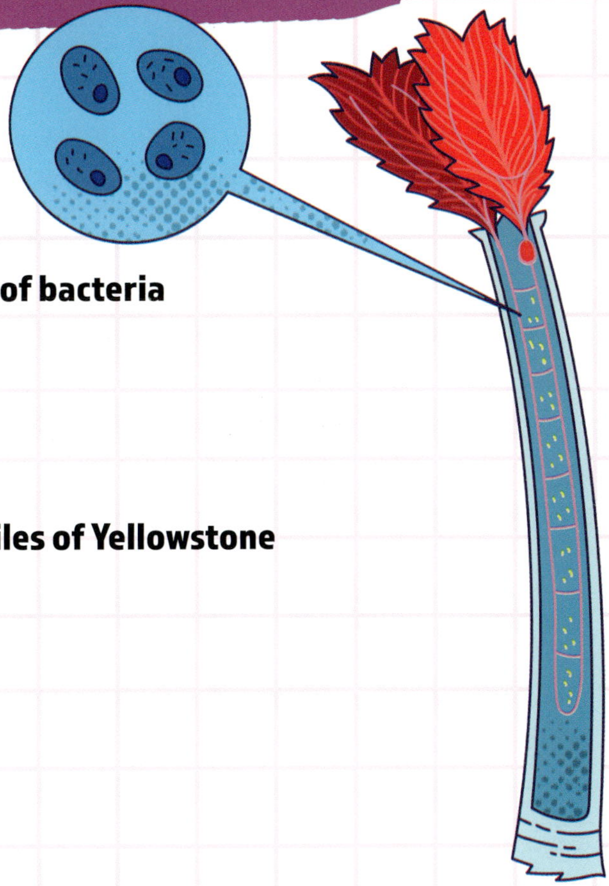

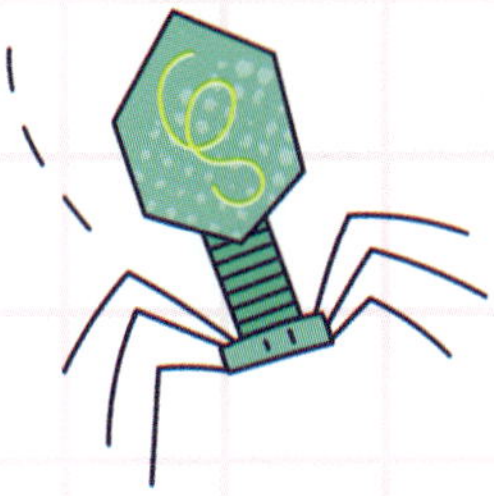

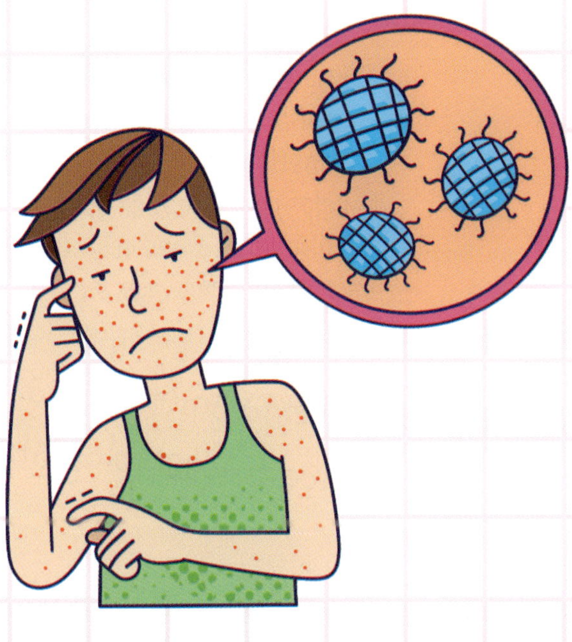

MEET THE BACTERIA

Wherever you are, there are billions of bacteria all around you. They're in the soil, in water, in your home, and in the air. They live on plants and animals, on you, and even inside your body. So what are they?

Pictures of bacteria often have bright colors added to make them easier to see.

Tiny life

Bacteria are tiny living things – so small, we can only see them with a microscope. Living things are made up of cells, and bacteria are single-celled. Each bacterium has just one very small cell.

This is a common bacterium called *Pseudomonas fluorescens*, found in soil and water.

In real life, it's much too small to see. You could fit a row of 500 of them into 1 millimeter on a ruler.

Many bacteria have tail-like parts, called flagella, which help them move around.

Bacteria science

Bacteriology is the science of bacteria. Studying bacteria is fascinating, but also useful – it helps us to treat illnesses, keep food safe, and use bacteria in new ways.

Bacteria scientists are called bacteriologists.

WHY DO THEY MATTER?

Bacteria are incredibly important in all kinds of ways. There are thousands of different species, or types, which do many different things.

- When living things die, bacteria feed on them, recycling useful chemicals into the soil.

- We use some types to make foods like cheese and yogurt.

- And some bacteria can make food decay and go bad.

- Some bacteria live inside animals, helping their bodies to work.

The *Pseudomonas fluorescens* on page 4 is one of them. If it starts growing in milk, it makes it go bad, smell awful, and taste sour.

- A few species of bacteria are germs that cause diseases and infections.

WE WERE HERE FIRST!

Bacteria were among the earliest life forms. They've been around for more than 3.5 BILLION years – much longer than humans!

THE WORLD OF BACTERIOLOGY

Bacteria may be tiny, but bacteriology is huge! It covers many ways of studying and working with bacteria, and links to lots of different areas of science.

Tiny science

Bacteriology is part of the larger science of microbiology. It's the study of tiny living things, or "microbes." While microbiologists study all kinds of microbes, such as viruses, yeast, and algae, bacteriologists just study bacteria.

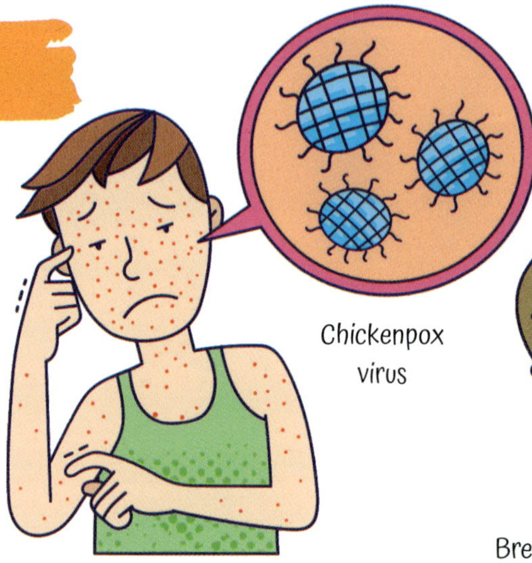

Some viruses cause diseases, such as chickenpox.

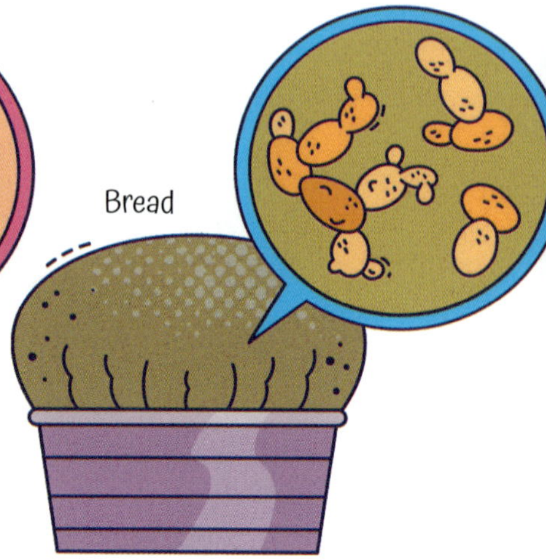

Bread yeast is a kind of single-celled fungus, and is related to mushrooms.

Viruses are tiny germs, even smaller than bacteria.

Name that science!

The names of sciences often end with "-ology." It's from the ancient Greek word *logos*, meaning discussions or words.

"Bacteria" is also from an ancient Greek word, meaning "little stick." That's because many bacteria are shaped like sticks, rods, or sausages (though they come in other shapes too).

In the lab

Bacteriologists often work in laboratories, or labs, in universities or research centers. They use microscopes to look closely at bacteria and do experiments on them to see how they grow, survive, and behave.

For example, imagine a new type of disease bacteria was discovered. Bacteriologists would do all kinds of studies and tests to find out more about it.

Here are some questions they would look into:

What kind of bacteria is it?
How fast does it grow?
Where does it like to live?
How does it get into people's bodies?
How does it make people sick?
Does boiling water kill it?
Does disinfectant kill it?
Can it survive in a freezer?

A microbiology lab full of microscopes and other science equipment

What else?

There are bacteriologists working in many other areas too. Their work includes:

- **Experimenting with bacteria to create new types of cheese or other foods**
- **Working for companies that make anti-bacterial chemicals or coatings**
- **Studying how people, plants, or animals are affected by bacteria.**

HOW BACTERIOLOGY BEGAN

One of the first people to see individual bacteria was a Dutch inventor, Antonie van Leeuwenhoek, in 1676. Using a powerful home-made microscope to look at pond water and tooth plaque, he saw tiny, moving creatures. From the 1700s onwards, other scientists began to study bacteria and find out more about them.

UNDERSTANDING BACTERIA

Before you can get started on some bacteria-based science, you need a few bacteria basics!

Take a look inside

This picture shows the main parts of a typical bacterium.

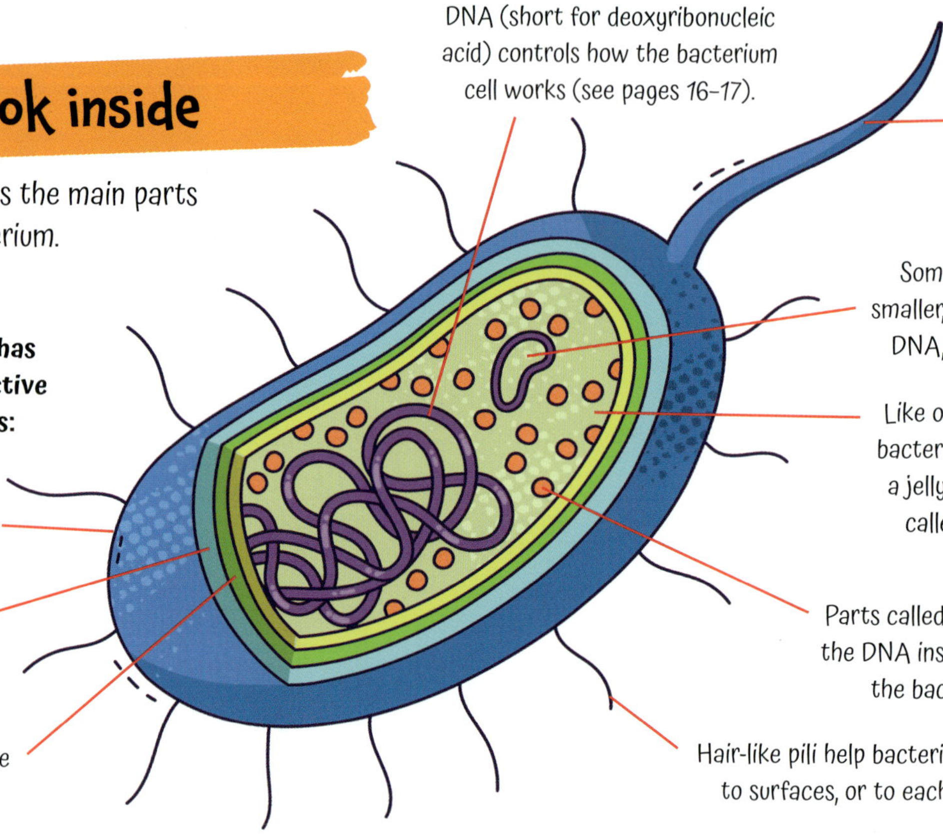

Spheres, sticks and spirals

Bacteria come in a variety of shapes, which can help scientists to identify them. The science of these shapes is called bacterial morphology.

- **Rod or stick-shaped bacteria**

Bacillus subtilis, found in soil, is harmless.

- **Spherical or ball-shaped bacteria**

Neisseria meningitidis, found in humans, can sometimes cause the disease meningitis.

- **Twisted or spiral-shaped bacteria**

Borrelia burgdorferi is spread in tick bites, and causes Lyme disease.

Naming bacteria

Like other living things, each bacteria species has a scientific name, written in Latin. That's why the bacteria in this book all have such strange-sounding names! For example, the bacteria in this picture are called *Vibrio cholerae*.

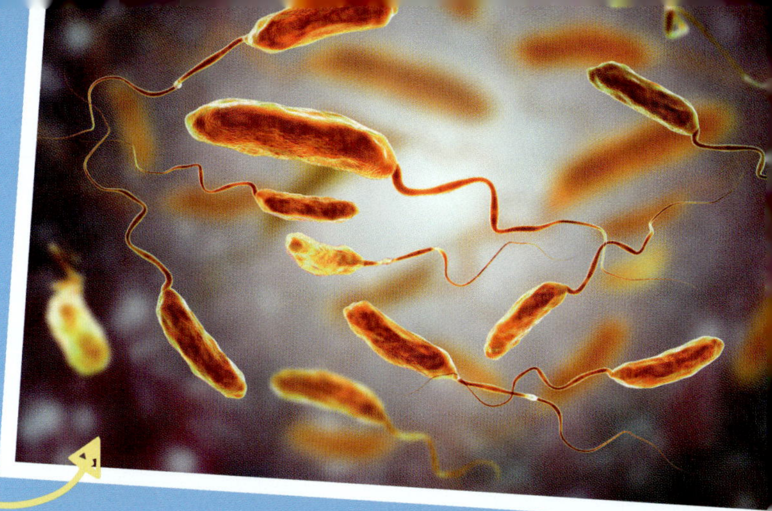

A Latin name usually has two parts:

The first part is the genus, or family name.

The second part describes something about the species. There are several *Vibrio* species.

Vibrio cholerae

"Vibrio" means tremble or vibrate, from the way these bacteria wiggle to and fro as they swim along.

The first part has a capital letter.

Scientific names are always written in *italics*!

The "cholerae" part means this is the bacterium that causes cholera, a dangerous disease.

HOW SMALL?

You've probably measured small things in millimeters – but bacteria are too tiny for that! Instead, bacteriologists measure them in micrometers. One micrometer is one-thousandth of a millimeter, and it's written like this:

µm

Most bacteria are between 1 and 10 µm long.

- **Sometimes, bacteria link themselves together in pairs, clusters or long chains.**

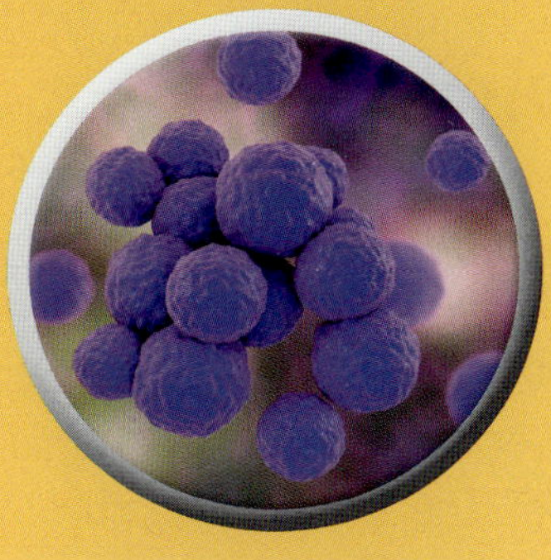

A cluster of *Staphylococcus aureus*, which is found on skin, can cause zits.

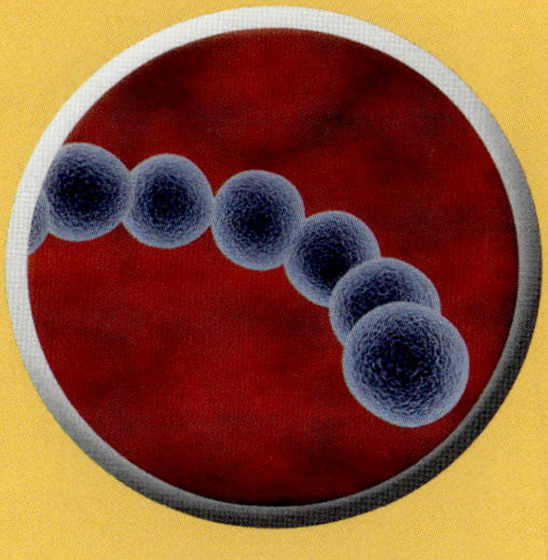

A chain of *Streptococcus* bacteria, which cause infections.

Case Study

E. coli, king of bacteria

If you ever study or work with bacteria, you'll see a lot of *E. coli*. It's the most famous, useful, experimented-on bacterium of them all.

It's inside you!

There are billions of *E. coli* bacteria living inside you right now. They are one of the many bacteria species that naturally live inside people's intestines, and inside other animals too. They feed on the food you eat, but also help your body by making useful vitamins, and keeping harmful bacteria away.

Gut bacteria such as *E. coli* are mainly found in the large intestine, or colon.

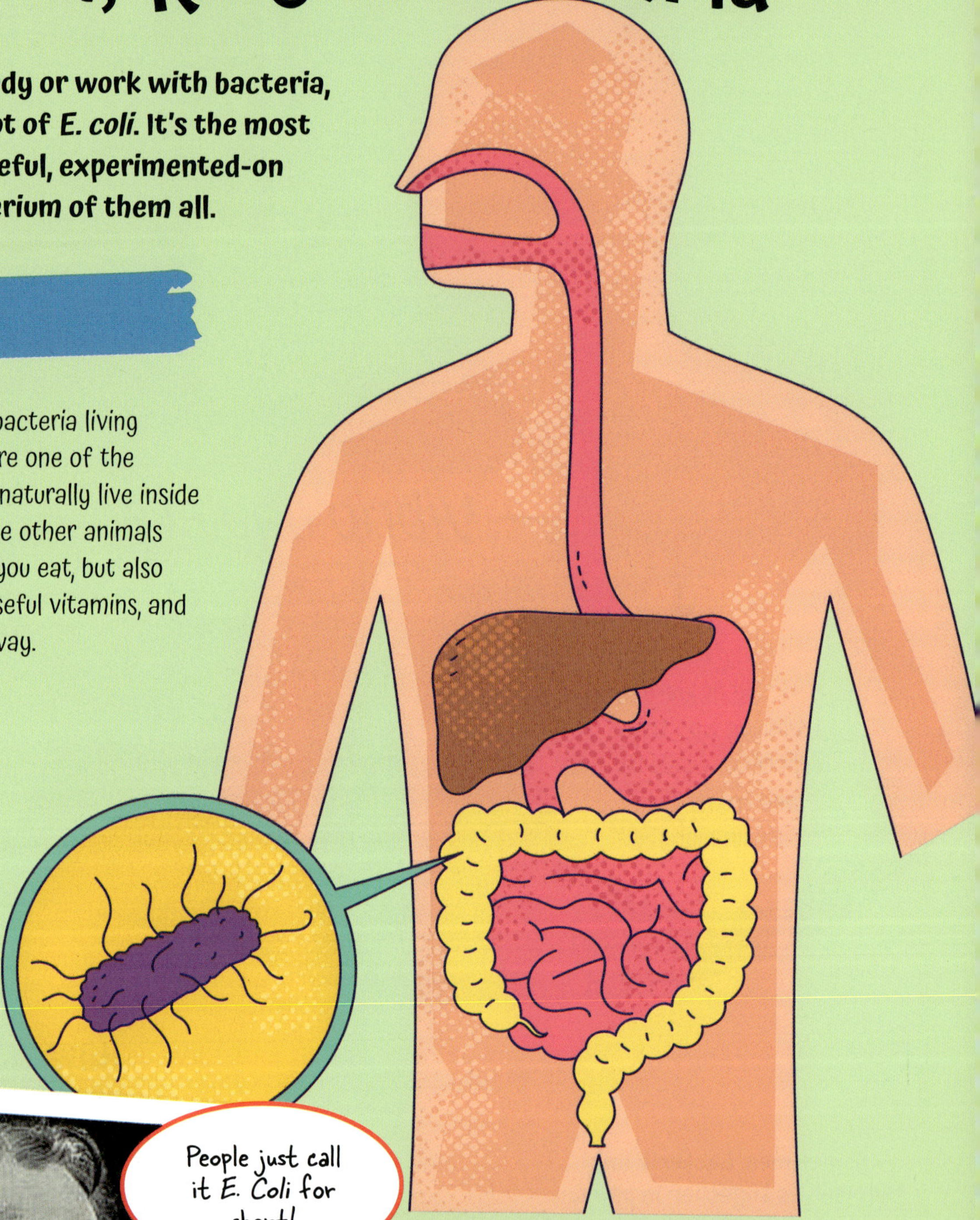

Poop pioneer

German doctor Theodor Escherich discovered *E. coli* in 1885, while studying germs in baby poop to see what caused illnesses. Later, it was named *Escherichia coli* after him. The "coli" part of the name is because it lives in the colon.

Science lab superstar

As more scientists began studying *E. coli*, they found it was very easy to work with.

- It grows fast and lives for a long time.
- It's easy to "culture" (or grow) in the lab.
- It's always easy to find, as it lives in humans.

Because of this, *E. coli* has been used for more experiments than any other species of bacteria. In fact, it's the most-studied, best understood living thing in the world.

Helpful and harmful

E. coli is normally harmless. But it can change and form different types, or strains, which can be harmful and cause illnesses.

When a person or animal poops, lots of living bacteria come out in the poop. This means that there are often *E. coli* bacteria in soil and water. If a harmful strain gets into food or drinking water, it can make people sick.

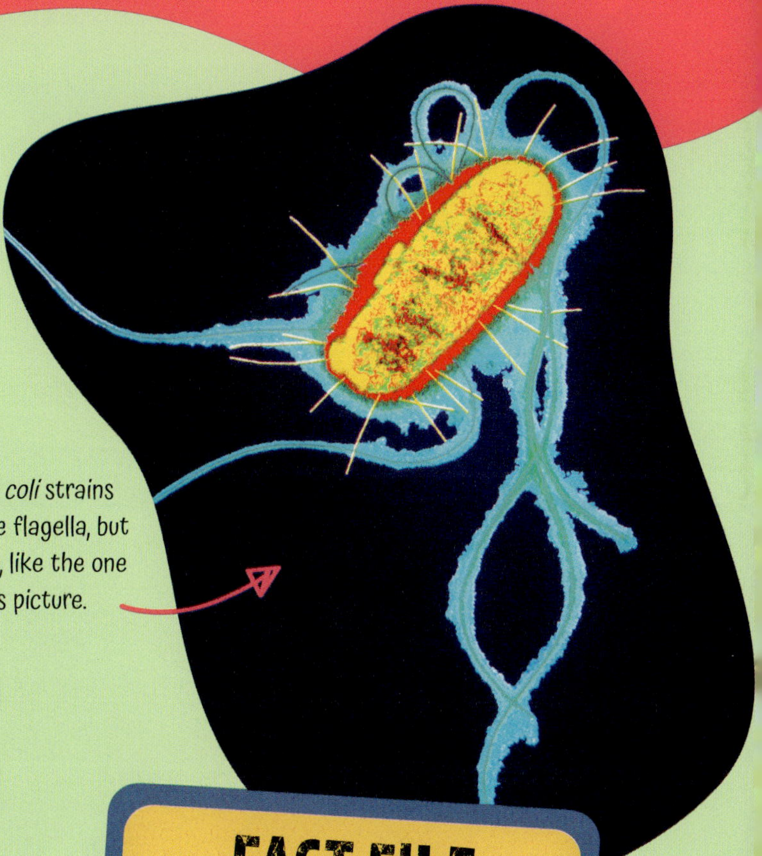

Some *E. coli* strains don't have flagella, but others do, like the one in this picture.

FACT FILE

NAME: ***ESCHERICHIA COLI***

DISCOVERED: 1885

DISCOVERER: THEODOR ESCHERICH

SHAPE: BACILLUS (ROD-SHAPED)

GRAM TYPE: GRAM-NEGATIVE (SEE PAGES 12–13)

SIZE: 2 μm LONG

WORKING WITH BACTERIA

How do bacteriologists find bacteria, identify them, and study them in the lab? Follow the steps to find out ...

1 Taking a sample

A bacteriologist collects a sample, such as some soil, and seals it inside a clean tube.

The bacteriologist takes a sample from one colony and puts it on a new agar plate to culture that particular species on its own.

4 Doing tests

Now the bacteriologist can look at the bacteria through a microscope to see what shape it is, and do other tests on it to identify it.

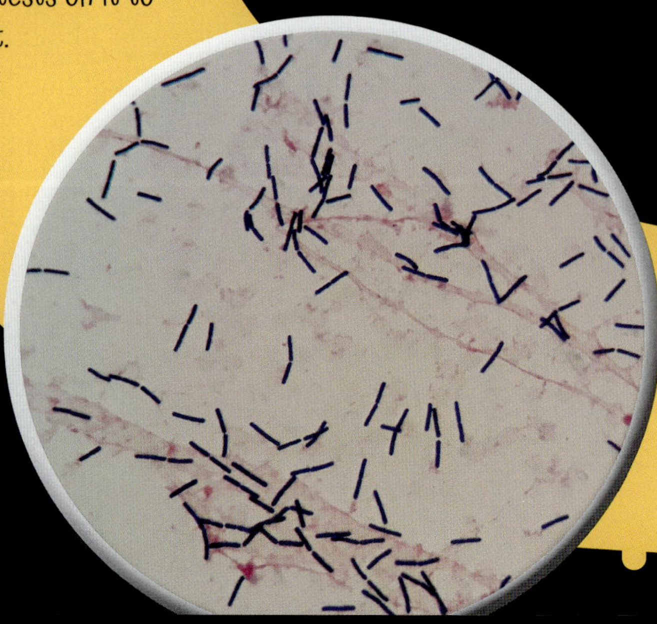

5 Pink or purple?

Scientists use a process called Gram staining to tell different bacteria apart.

They soak bacteria with purple chemicals, then wash them with another chemical.

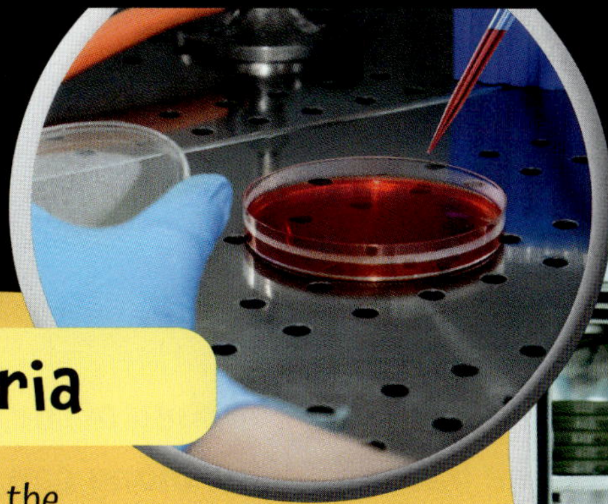

2 Culturing the bacteria

The sample is mixed with water, then the bacteriologist spreads a drop of the water onto an agar plate. This is a small dish called a petri dish, filled with agar jelly that bacteria can grow on.

The plate goes into an incubator, which keeps it at a medium-warm temperature. This cultures the bacteria, or helps them to grow.

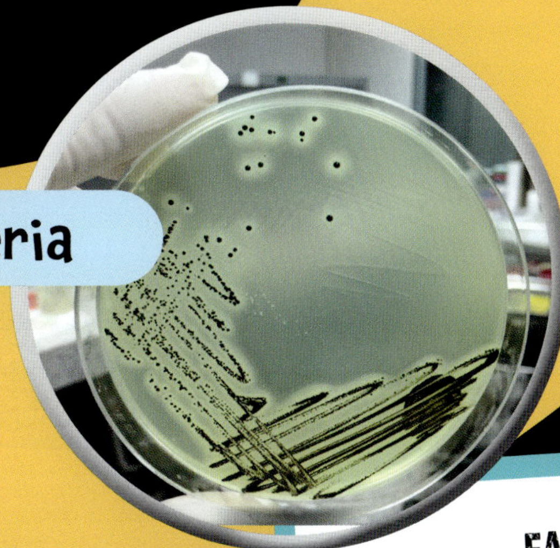

3 Isolating bacteria

Over 2-3 days, the bacteria reproduce and grow into groups, or colonies, which appear as little blobs.

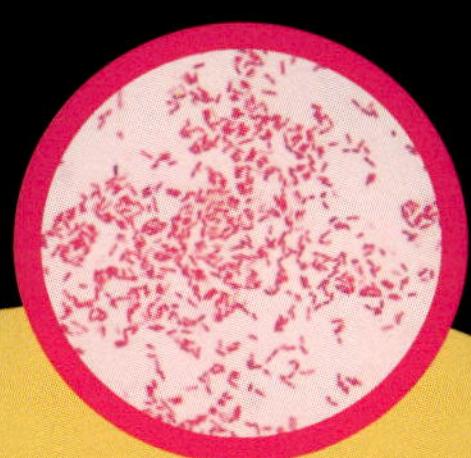

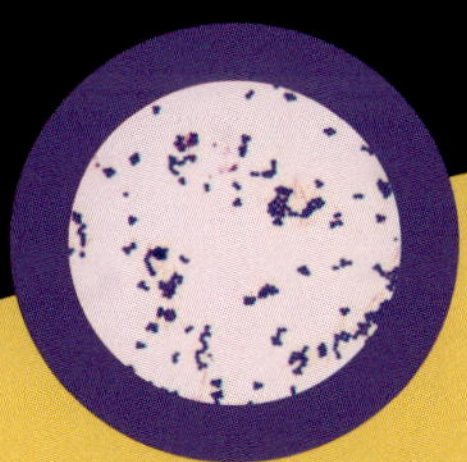

Gram-negative bacteria have thinner cell walls that don't hold as much dye.

They look pink.

Gram-positive bacteria have thick cell walls that tightly hold onto the dye.

They look purple through a microscope.

FANNY HESSE

Bacteriologists use agar plates thanks to Fanny Hesse. She was the wife of German microbiologist Walther Hesse, and often helped him with his work. In 1881, she suggested that agar, which she used in cooking, would be better for growing bacteria than gelatin, which melted in warm weather. It worked brilliantly and has been used ever since.

LIVING TOGETHER

Bacteria have only one cell each, but they often live together in a colony. The bacteria in a colony can even "talk" to each other!

One becomes many

If a bacterium has enough food, and good conditions (such as the right temperature), it will reproduce and make more bacteria. Bacteria do this by dividing, or splitting in two. This process is known as binary fission.

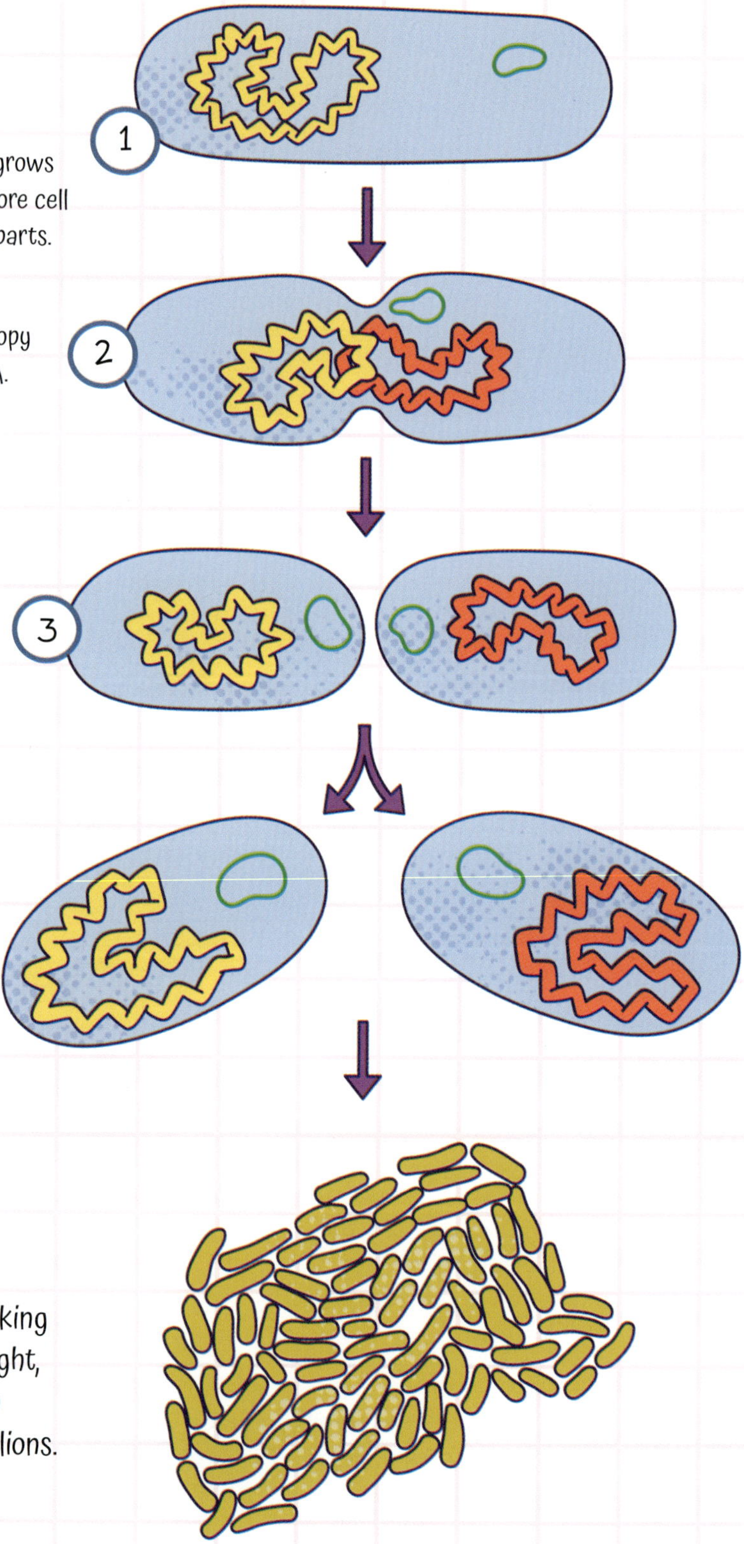

1. The bacterium grows bigger, building more cell wall and other parts.
2. It makes a copy of its DNA.
3. It separates into two new bacteria, each with its own parts and DNA.

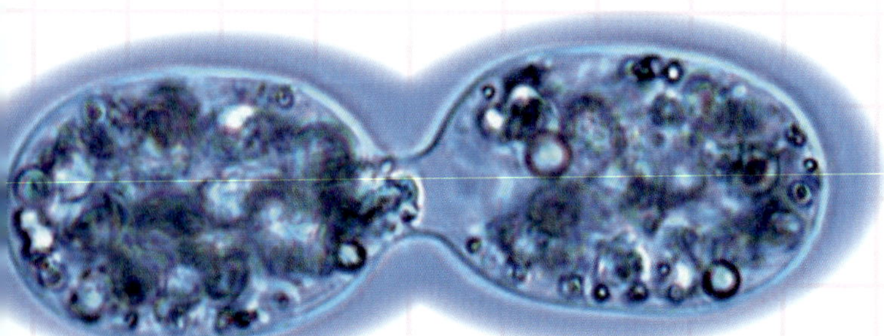

A *klebsiella pneumoniae* bacterium dividing

Then the new bacteria divide as well, making four bacteria. They also divide, making eight, and so on. In this way, one bacterium can quickly become a colony of millions or billions.

Chemical chatting

In 1970, bacteriologists working with bioluminescent (glowing) bacteria noticed something interesting. The bacteria didn't glow on their own, or when a colony started to grow. But when a large colony had formed, they did glow. Why?

They realized that the bacteria could somehow send a signal to each other. This is now known as quorum sensing.

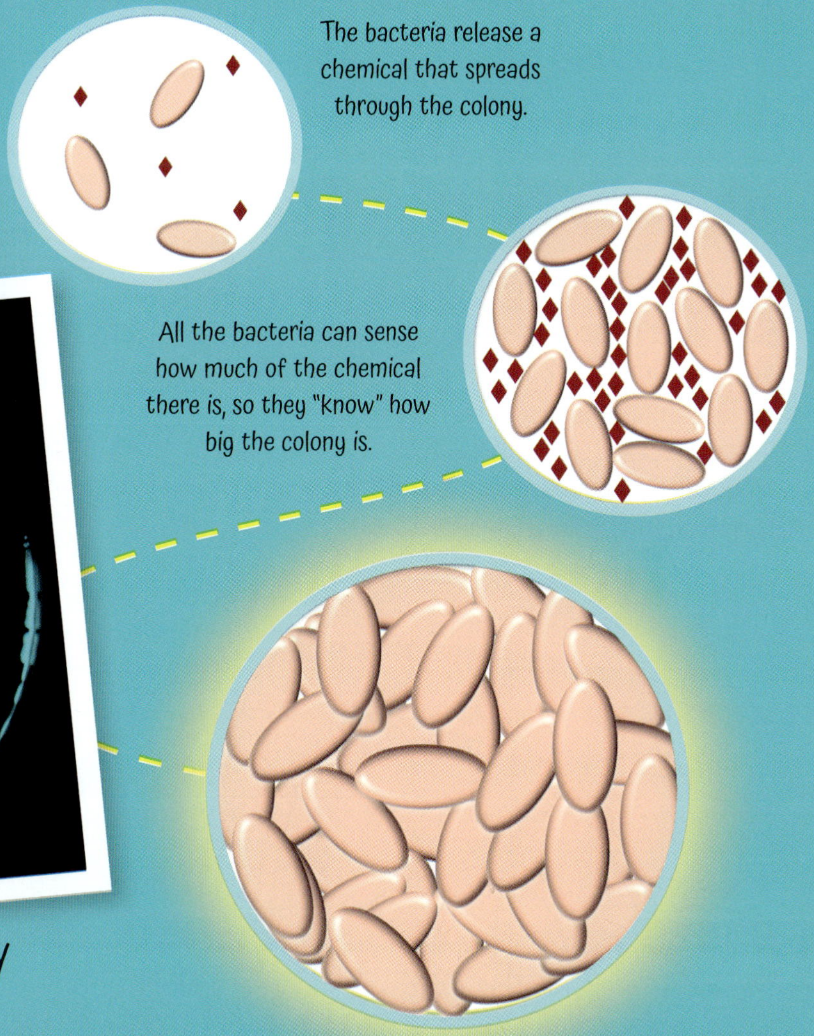

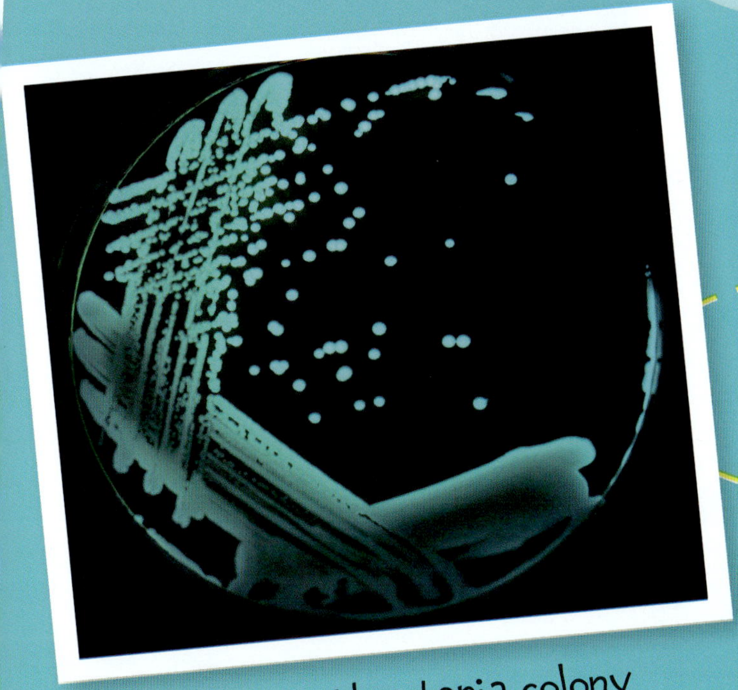

A glowing bacteria colony

WOLF PACK

One type of soil bacteria, called *Myxococcus xanthus*, goes hunting in a group, known as a "wolf pack." When the bacteria sense they are in a group, they glide forwards, releasing chemicals that kill other bacteria, which they then feed on.

IN THE GENES

Like humans, and other living things, bacteria have genes and DNA. They control how a bacterium grows and lives.

What are genes and DNA?

Genes are instructions that tell living cells how to work. Each gene is made of a sequence of chemicals that act like a code. Other parts of the cell "read" the code to make useful substances the cell needs.

DNA is what genes are made of. It's a long, string-shaped chemical.

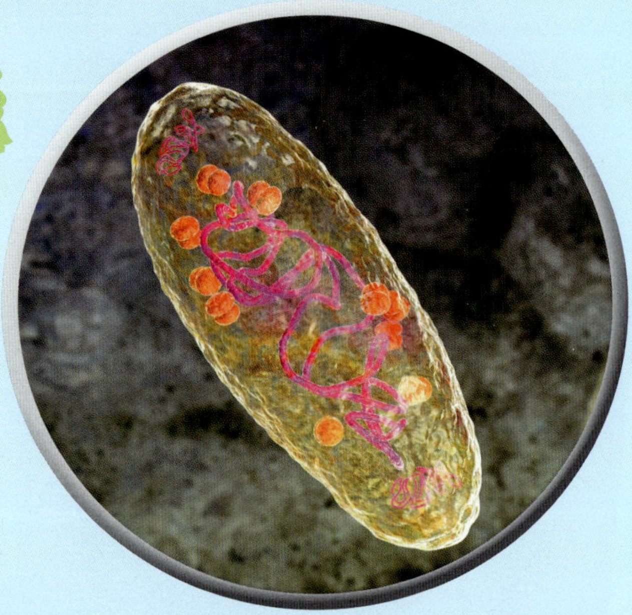

In this microscope image, you can see the DNA inside a bacterium.

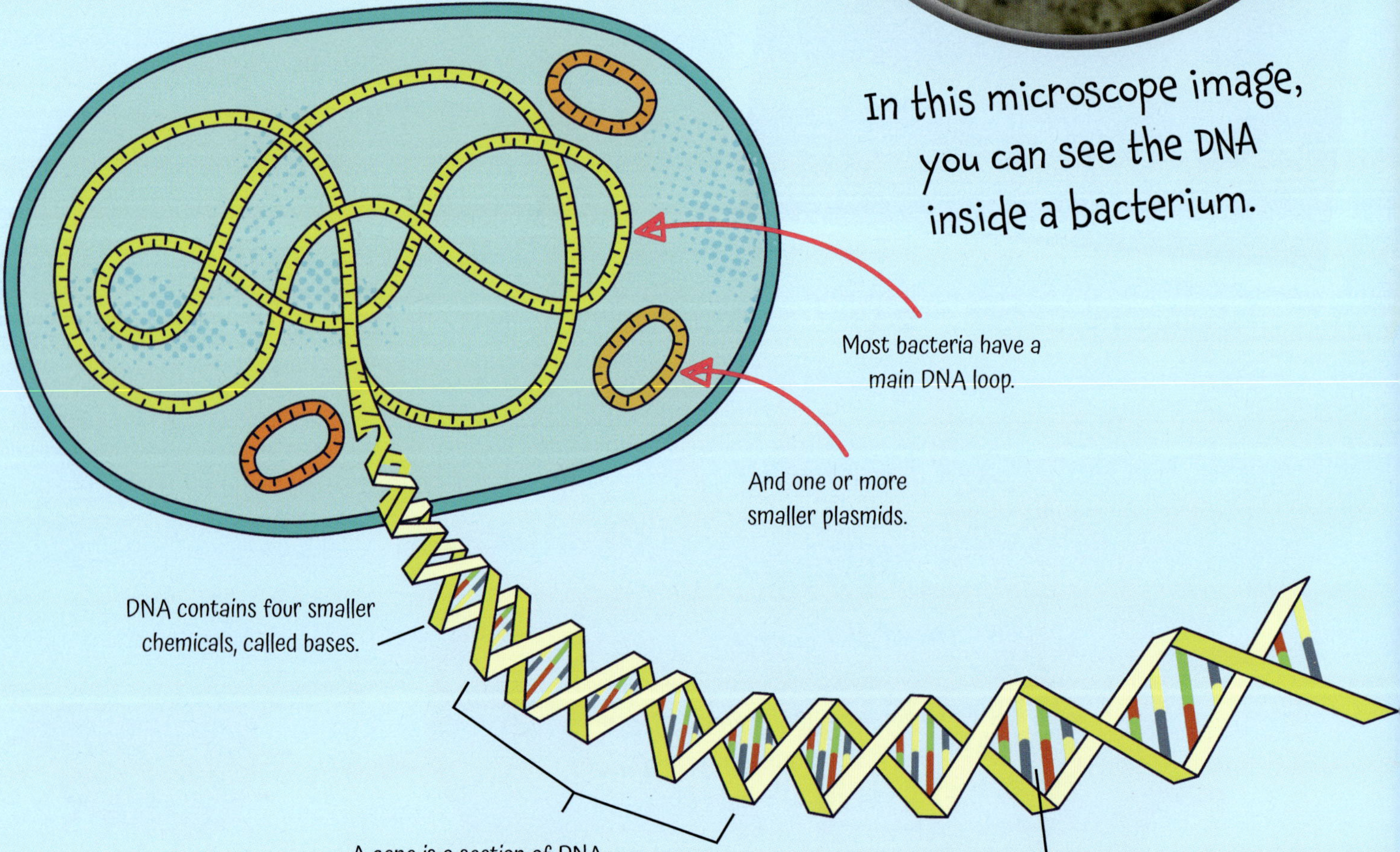

Changing over time

When bacteria divide to make more bacteria, they copy and pass on their DNA and genes. Sometimes, mistakes happen in the copying, making new, slightly different bacteria with different genes.

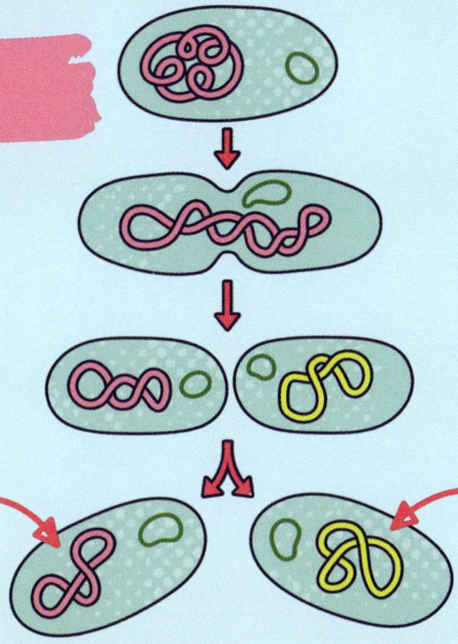

These new genes might be useful, making the bacterium better at surviving. And if the new bacterium is good at surviving, it will divide and make more bacteria like itself. In this way, bacteria evolve, or change over time, and form new strains, or types.

Tracking the changes

Studying new strains of bacteria is important for keeping track of disease germs. For example, a medicine that works on an old strain might not work on a new strain. Or a new strain might have features that make it more dangerous.

Understanding new strains helps us make new medicines that work to keep diseases under control.

HERE, HAVE THIS!

Bacteria have another cunning trick too – they can share or swap DNA.

If a bacterium has a useful plasmid, it can copy it and pass it to another bacterium that doesn't have one, using a special tube.

Case Study

Extremophiles of Yellowstone

In 1964, microbiology professor Thomas Brock visited Yellowstone National Park in Wyoming. He was amazed to see that the boiling hot springs there seemed to have something living in them.

Testing the water

Brock began to study the hot spring water to see what lived in it, along with his colleague Hudson Freeze. They left glass microscope slides in the water so that any bacteria in the water could stick to them, then looked at them under the microscope.

Thermal springs at Yellowstone National Park, containing extremophile bacteria that give them their bright colors

A new species

Brock and Freeze found various types of bacteria, including a new species previously unknown to science. They named it *Thermus aquaticus*, meaning "hot water", as it could live at 176°F (80°C). That's much hotter than a hot bath and would burn a human.

AT THE EXTREMES

Until then, scientists had thought that no living thing could survive in water this hot. The discovery showed that some bacteria have amazing abilities to thrive in extra-tough conditions that would kill most living things. They are now known as extremophiles, or "lovers of extremes." As well as bacteria that like extreme heat, many other types have been discovered.

Thermophile
Heat-loving

Acidophile
Acid-loving

Halophile
Salt-loving

Cryophile
Cold-loving

Xerophile
Dryness-loving

HIGH-SPEED TESTING

The discovery of *Thermus aquaticus* led to another huge change in science. A heat-resistant chemical from the new bacteria was used to develop a way of copying DNA quickly at high temperatures, called PCR (Polymerase Chain Reaction). It's used in DNA sequencing and testing, and tests for diseases.

PCR tests are used to test for COVID-19 by identifying the genes in the virus.

FACT FILE

NAME: ***THERMUS AQUATICUS***

DISCOVERED: 1969

SHAPE: BACILLUS (ROD-SHAPED)

GRAM TYPE: GRAM-NEGATIVE

SIZE: 5-10 µm LONG

BACTERIA AND DISEASES

Most bacteria do not cause diseases. But a few do, and they can cause big problems. Bacteriologists play an important part in studying and helping to control them.

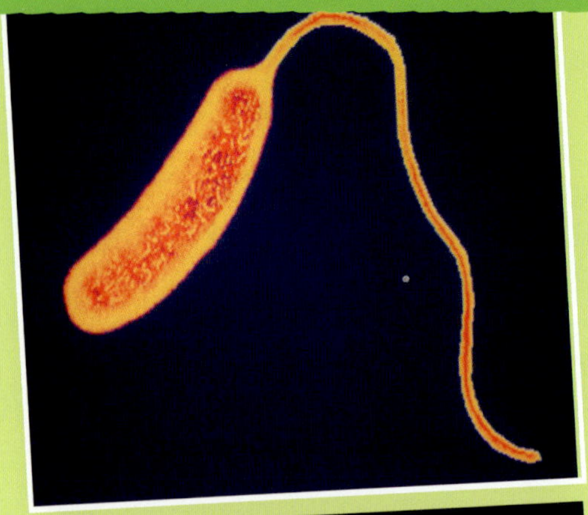

Cholera

Caused by: *Vibrio cholerae*
Effects: Severe diarrhea and vomiting

A killer in places without sewage systems and clean water.

Disease bugs

Here are some of the serious, sometimes deadly, diseases caused by bacteria.

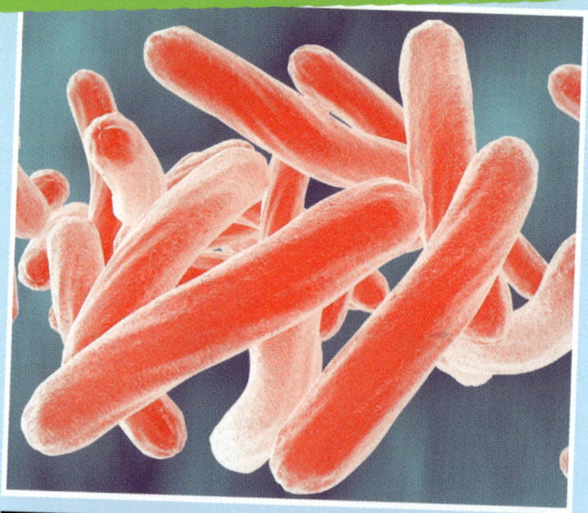

TB (short for tuberculosis)

Caused by: *Mycobacterium tuberculosis*
Effects: Damages lungs or other body parts, can be fatal

Over 10 million people get sick with TB every year.

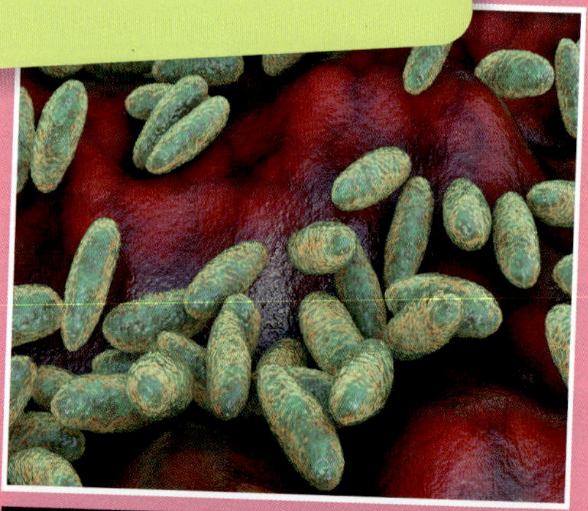

Plague (or the Black Death)

Caused by: *Yersinia pestis*
Effects: Swelling, blotchy skin, coughing and weakness

Before modern medicines, outbreaks of plague killed millions of people.

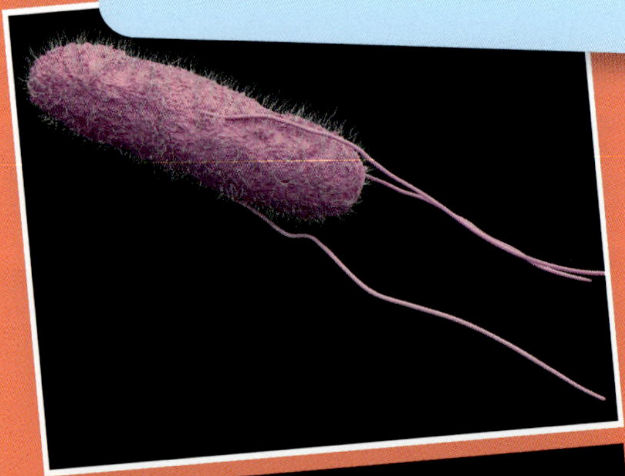

Infections

There are also many types of bacteria that can cause problems if they infect you or start growing in your body. Earaches, food poisoning, acne, and meningitis, for example, can be caused by various different bacteria species.

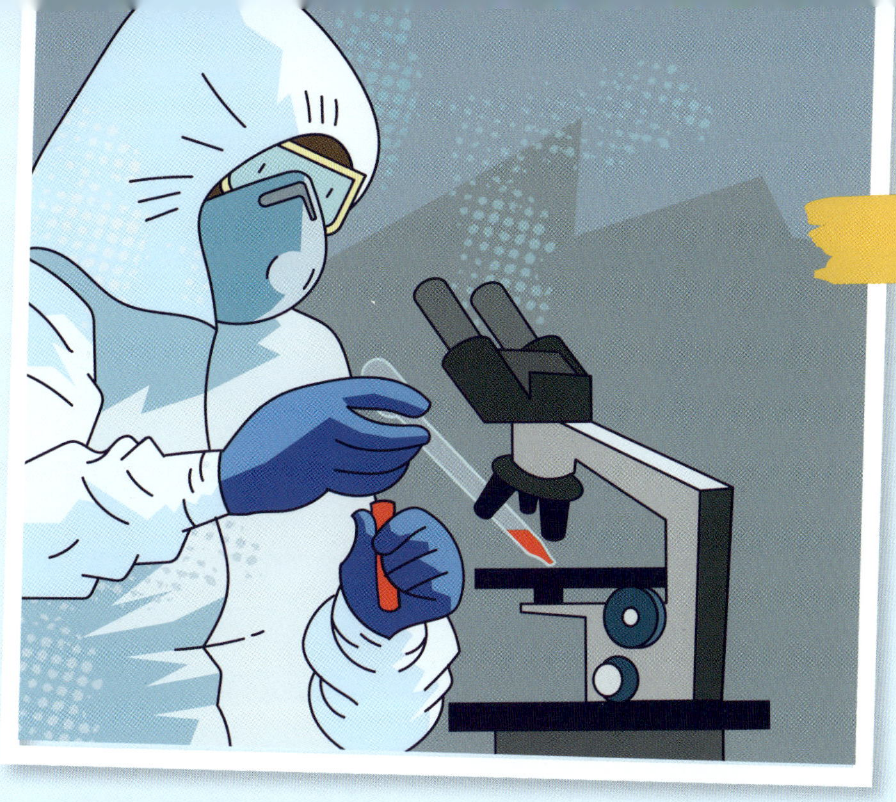

Working with germs

Bacteriologists study disease bacteria in many ways:

- **Doing tests to look for bacteria species, for example, in a water supply**
- **Studying how bacteria harm the body, or spread between people**
- **Inventing new bacteria-killing medicines, and testing them to see what works best.**

When working with dangerous bacteria, scientists wear protective gear to make sure they don't get infected themselves.

Germ theory

Germ theory is the idea that germs cause diseases.

- **Even in ancient times, some people thought diseases might be spread by tiny creatures.**
- **In the 1700s, scientists began studying bacteria with microscopes.**
- **In 1854, Dr. John Snow showed how cholera was spread by germs in dirty water.**
- **In the late 1800s, bacteriologists such as Louis Pasteur and Robert Koch did experiments that linked bacteria species to the diseases they caused.**

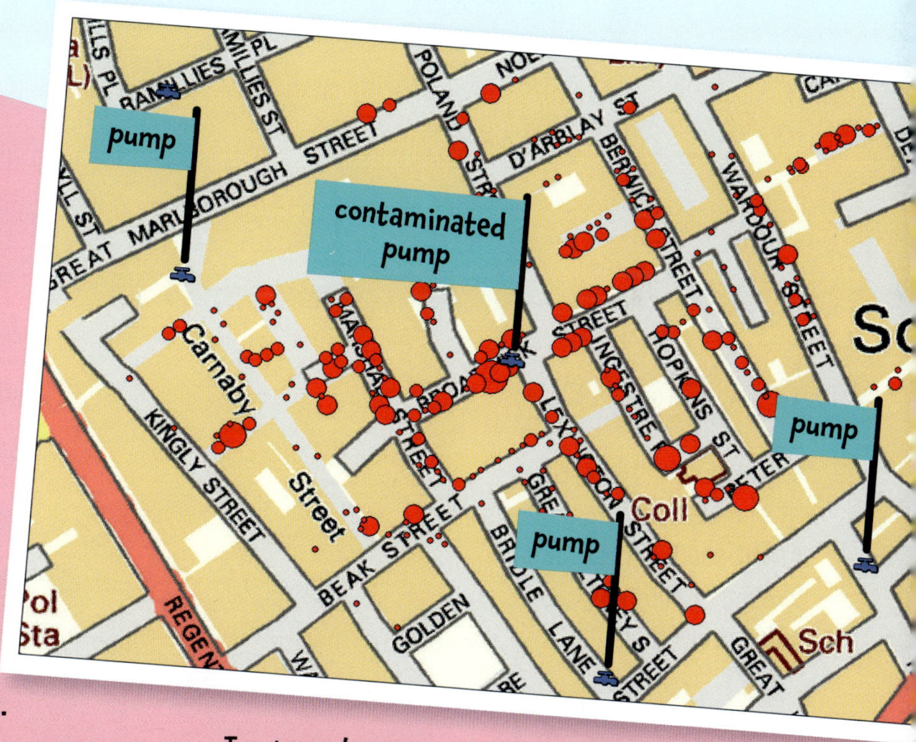

In London, UK, John Snow found that cholera cases were clustered around a single water pump, which was contaminated with bacteria.

BANISHING BACTERIA

One way to stay safe from harmful bacteria is to get rid of them *before* they can get into our bodies and cause illnesses.

Food products such as milk, ice cream, and honey are often pasteurized, or heated to kill germs. It's named after bacteria expert Louis Pasteur, who discovered it in the 1860s.

Food safety

Strict rules for preparing food keep us safe from food poisoning bacteria.

For example, keeping meat in a fridge or freezer stops bacteria from growing.

Food preparation areas and tools must be clean and washed after use.

Cooking meat all the way through kills bacteria.

Keep it clean

We also keep bacteria at bay by cleaning. It might sound simple, but everyday cleaning saves millions of lives.

• Sanitation means things like running water, flushing toilets, hot showers, and sewage systems that filter and clean the water we use.

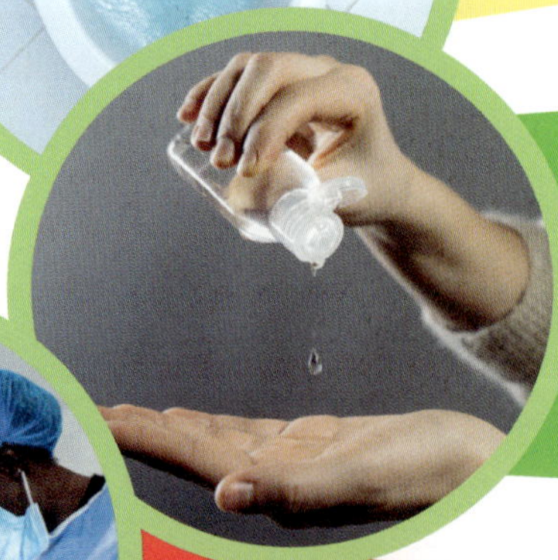

• We use antiseptics, or bacteria-killing chemicals, to clean homes, schools, and factories; in hand sanitizers; and in swimming pools.

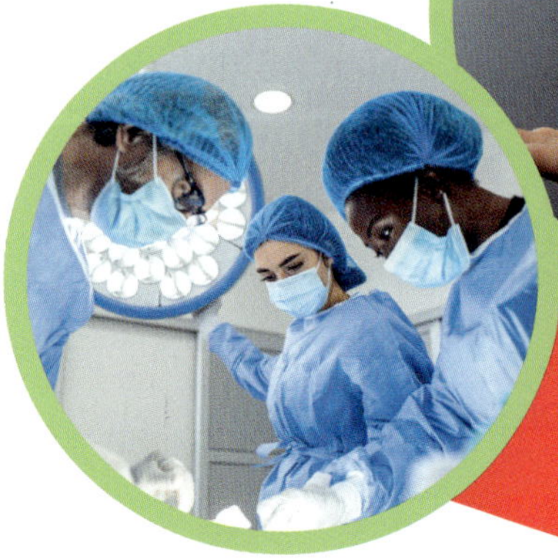

• Hospitals have to be very clean, especially in operating rooms, where germs could get into your body.

Keeping up

Some bacteriologists work on antibacterial chemicals and processes, and keep track of how well they work. For example, they might find a new strain of *Salmonella* that's heat-resistant, meaning it has to be heated at a higher temperature to kill it.

Things like sewage systems and pasteurization cost money. That means they are less common in poorer countries, so people there are more at risk of bacterial diseases.

Handwashing hero

Florence Nightingale, a nurse in British army hospitals in the 1850s, saw that injured soldiers were mainly dying from diseases they caught in the hospital. She changed this by keeping the wards clean and making sure the nurses washed their hands.

Nightingale made pie charts to demonstrate her discoveries, and wrote books on how to run hospitals.

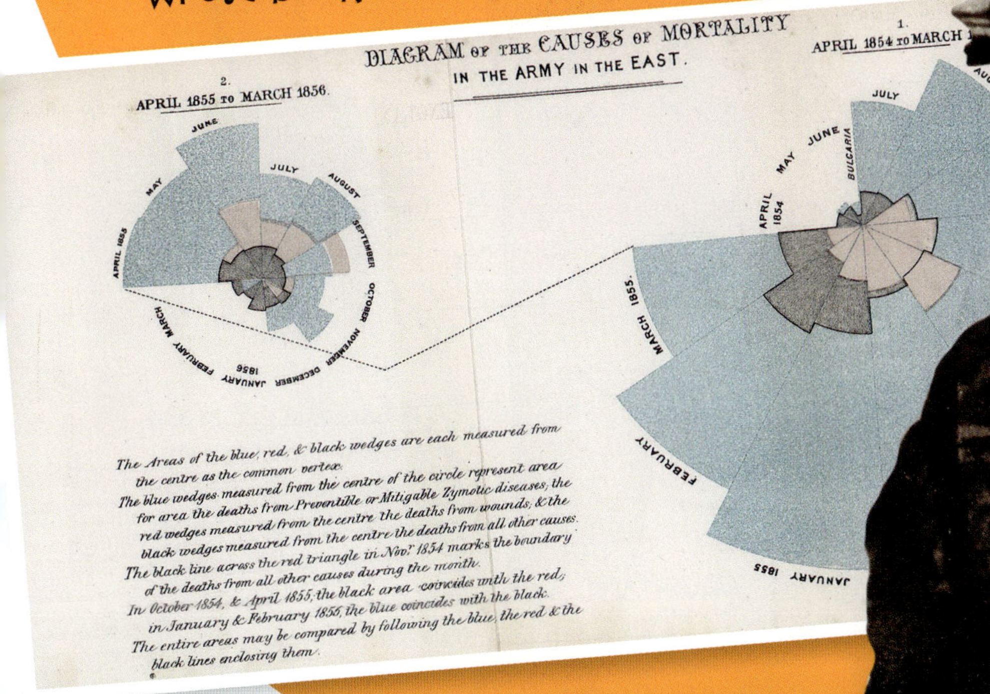

THE IMMUNE SYSTEM

We've been living alongside disease bacteria for millions of years. Over time, our bodies have evolved to fight them.

Your antibacterial body

The human body's immune system, or disease-fighting system, has several ways to keep bacteria out, or kill them if they get in.

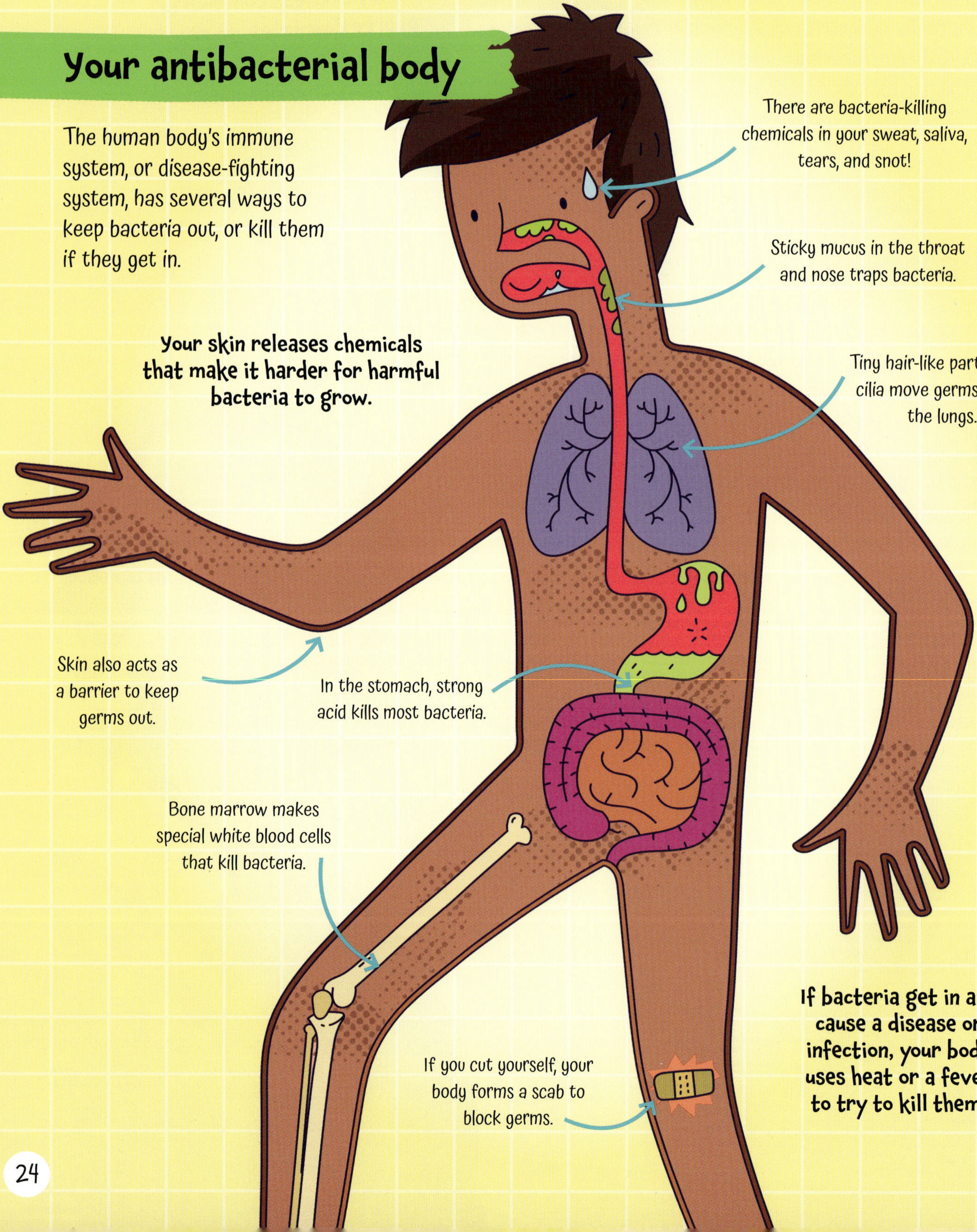

STUDYING TEARS

Bacteriologists are still discovering new antibacterial chemicals in human tears. They could eventually be copied and used to make new bacteria-killing medicines or food additives.

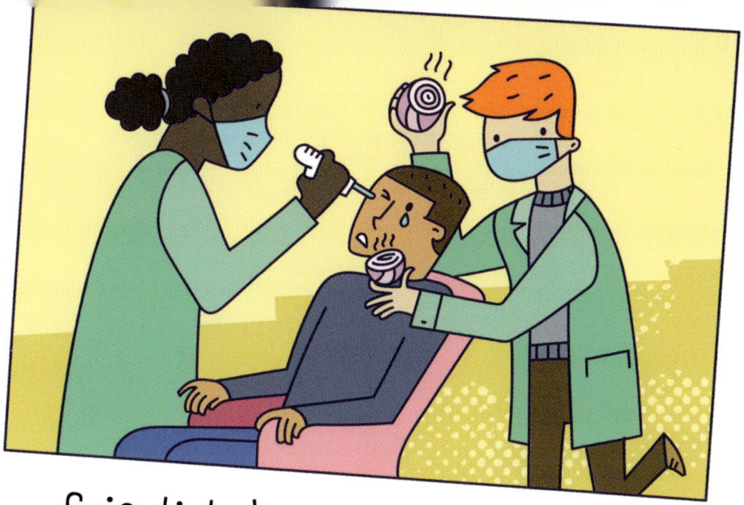

Scientists have to collect human tears to study.

Vaccinations

The immune system can learn to fight particular bacteria species. For example, if you've had whooping cough, your immune system learns to recognize the bacteria that cause it, so you're less likely to get it again.

A vaccine works by giving you a partial or weakened version of a disease germ, so that you don't get the disease, but your immune system still learns to fight it. Vaccinations for viruses have been used since medieval times, but it wasn't until the late 1800s that Louis Pasteur created the first vaccine against a bacterial disease – chicken cholera!

EWW, THAT'S REVOLTING!

If you see a dog poop or some vomit, you try to avoid them. That's because humans have evolved to find these things disgusting. This makes us keep away from them, and avoid harmful bacteria.

New discoveries

Since the late 1800s, bacteriologists have invented vaccines for more bacterial diseases, including TB, cholera, plague, and whooping cough. But they're still working on new ones – such as new, better TB vaccines, and cheaper vaccines that all countries can afford.

ANTIBIOTICS

If you do get a bacterial disease or infection, you'll probably get better, thanks to antibiotics. These amazing medicines have saved millions of lives.

What have you got?

If a doctor doesn't know what bacteria are making you ill, they take some blood, or a swab from a wound, and send it off to a bacteriology lab. There the bacteriologists grow a culture (see page 11), then do tests to identify the culprit.

Once the bacteria are identified, you can take the right antibiotics. But what are they?

Germ-killers

Antibiotics are chemicals that kill bacteria, or stop them from growing. They can be human-made, but often come from other living things, especially molds, which make them to fight off bacteria themselves.

In the late 1800s, German doctor Paul Erlich developed early antibiotics, using chemicals he found in dyes. Meanwhile, scientists noticed that some molds could kill bacteria too.

The ancient Egyptians knew that moldy bread could help wounds to heal.

It was actually the antibiotic chemicals being released by the mold that were killing the germs.

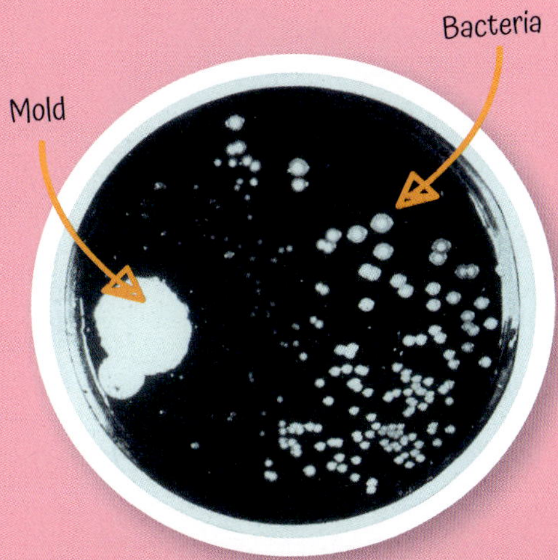

Fleming's famous petri dish

Then, in 1928, Scottish scientist Alexander Fleming found that mold growing on an old, unwashed petri dish had killed the bacteria around it. The mold was releasing a bacteria-zapping chemical, which he called penicillin.

From about 1945, penicillin was widely used as a medicine, and bacteriologists studied lots more molds and other living things to find more antibiotics.

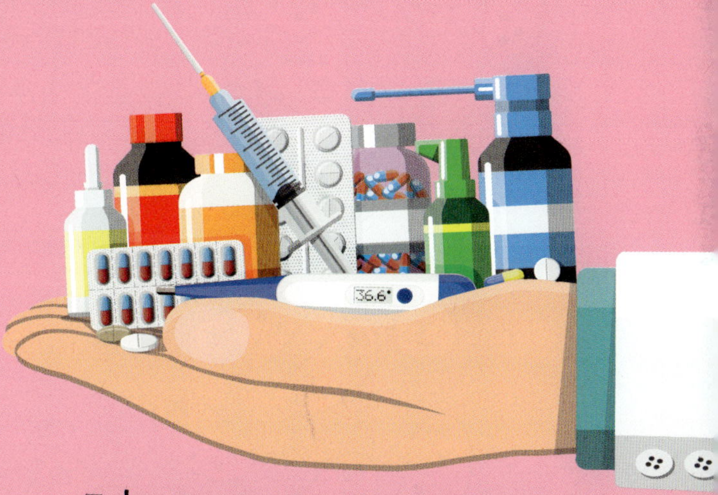

Today, we use over 100 antibiotics against different types of bacteria.

MOLDY MARY

It took years to turn penicillin into an everyday medicine, because the first mold it was found in did not make enough of it. American bacteriologist, Mary Hunt, solved the problem in 1943, when she found a new mold growing on a melon in a market, which produced much more penicillin – earning her the nickname "Moldy Mary."

ANTIBIOTIC RESISTANCE

Unfortunately, there's a problem with antibiotics – a BIG problem. The bacteria are fighting back!

Evolving resistance

Bacteria can evolve and change quickly (see page 17). This means they can sometimes evolve resistance to an antibiotic so that it can't kill them.

Here's how it works:

1

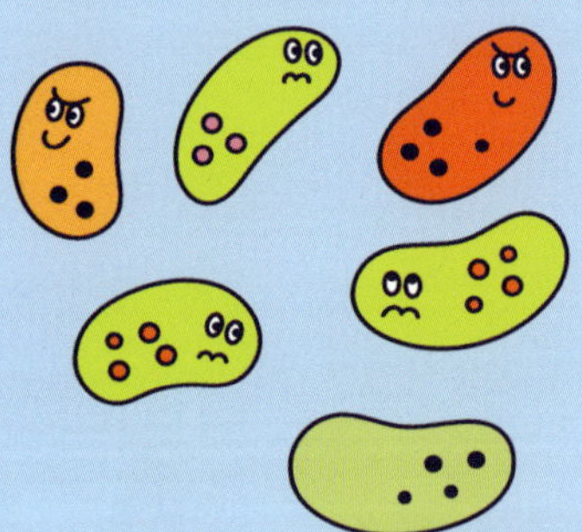

An antibiotic kills most of the bacteria, but a few have DNA changes that help them live longer.

2

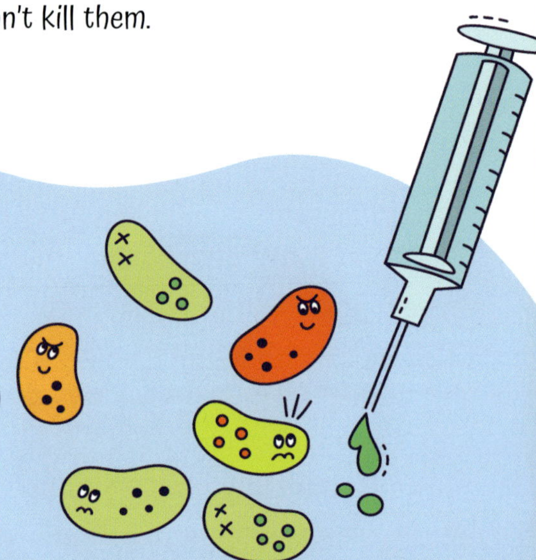

If the antibiotic isn't used for long enough, the super-tough bacteria survive.

3

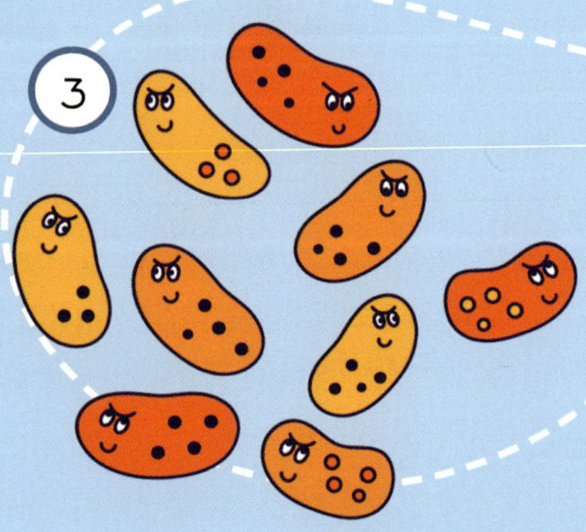

Now there's space for these bacteria to grow and multiply, becoming a new, antibiotic-resistant strain.

4

Even worse, bacteria can share useful DNA (see page 17). The resistant bacteria give copies of their DNA to other bacteria, so more become resistant.

What could happen?

There are now several types of harmful bacteria that antibiotics don't work on, sometimes called "superbugs." They include some strains of TB, and MRSA (methicillin-resistant *Staphylococcus aureus*), which sometimes spreads in hospitals.

This means we could return to the days before antibiotics, when many more people died from bacterial diseases like TB, or from infections in cuts or wounds.

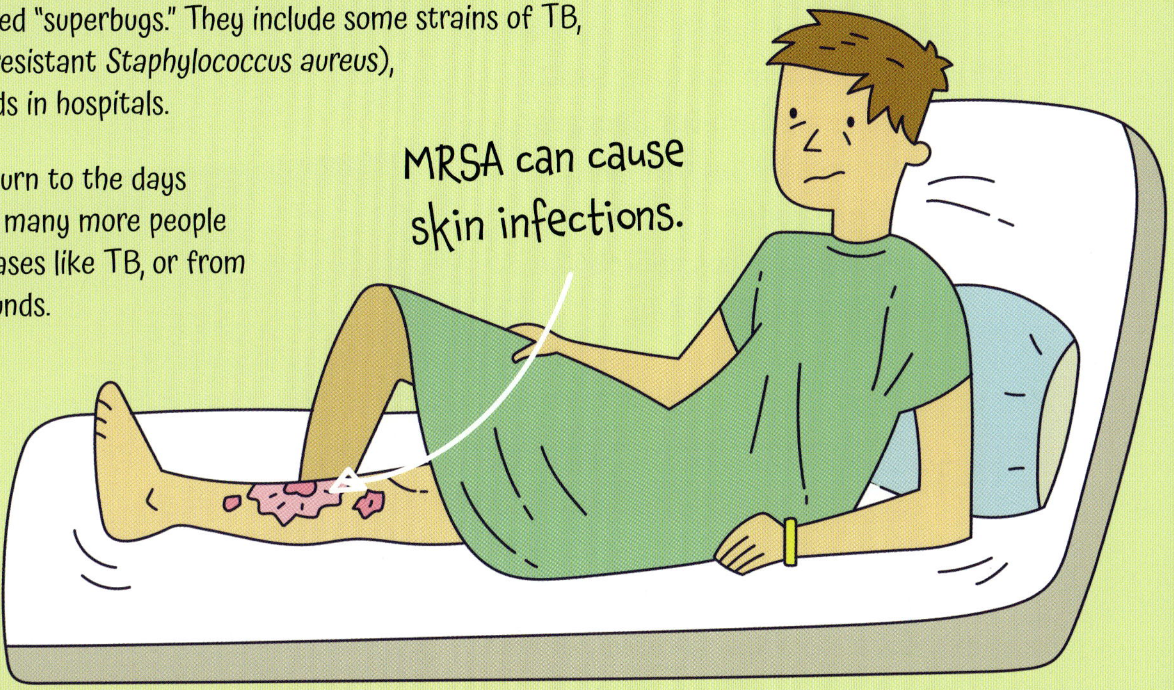

BACTERIOLOGY TO THE RESCUE!

But don't panic – bacteriologists are hard at work trying to find solutions. They include ...

- **Looking for previously unknown molds, or other living things, that we could use to make new types of antibiotics. They're looking in all kinds of places ...**

- **Developing new drugs called host-directed therapies (HDTs) that make our bodies better at fighting bacteria.**
- **Using viruses that attack bacteria, called bacteriophages, as medicines** **(see pages 30–31).**

KEEP TAKING THE MEDICINE!

Even if you're not a bacteriologist, you can help. If a doctor gives you antibiotics, always take them for as long as you're told to. Stopping too soon (even if you feel better) makes it easier for resistant bacteria to evolve.

Case Study

Phage Muddy

In 2010, students in Durban, South Africa, were searching for bacteria-killing viruses as part of their classes. One student, Lilli Holst, discovered a new virus, which she named Phage Muddy.

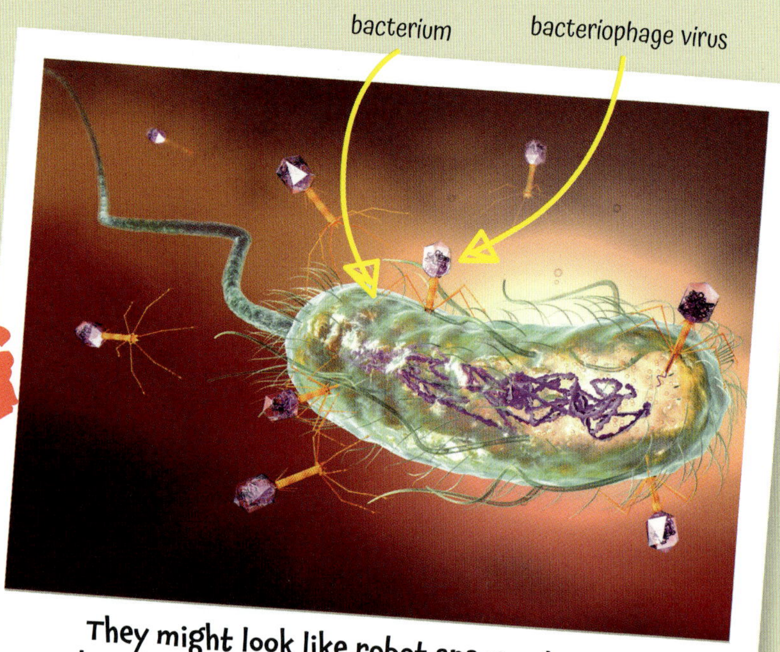

They might look like robot space octopuses, but these are actually bacteriophage viruses attacking a bacterium.

Bacteria-eaters

While some viruses attack human, animal, or plant cells, others only attack bacteria. They are called phages, or bacteriophages, meaning "bacteria eaters."

How viruses work

Viruses are tiny, and can only live by invading living cells.

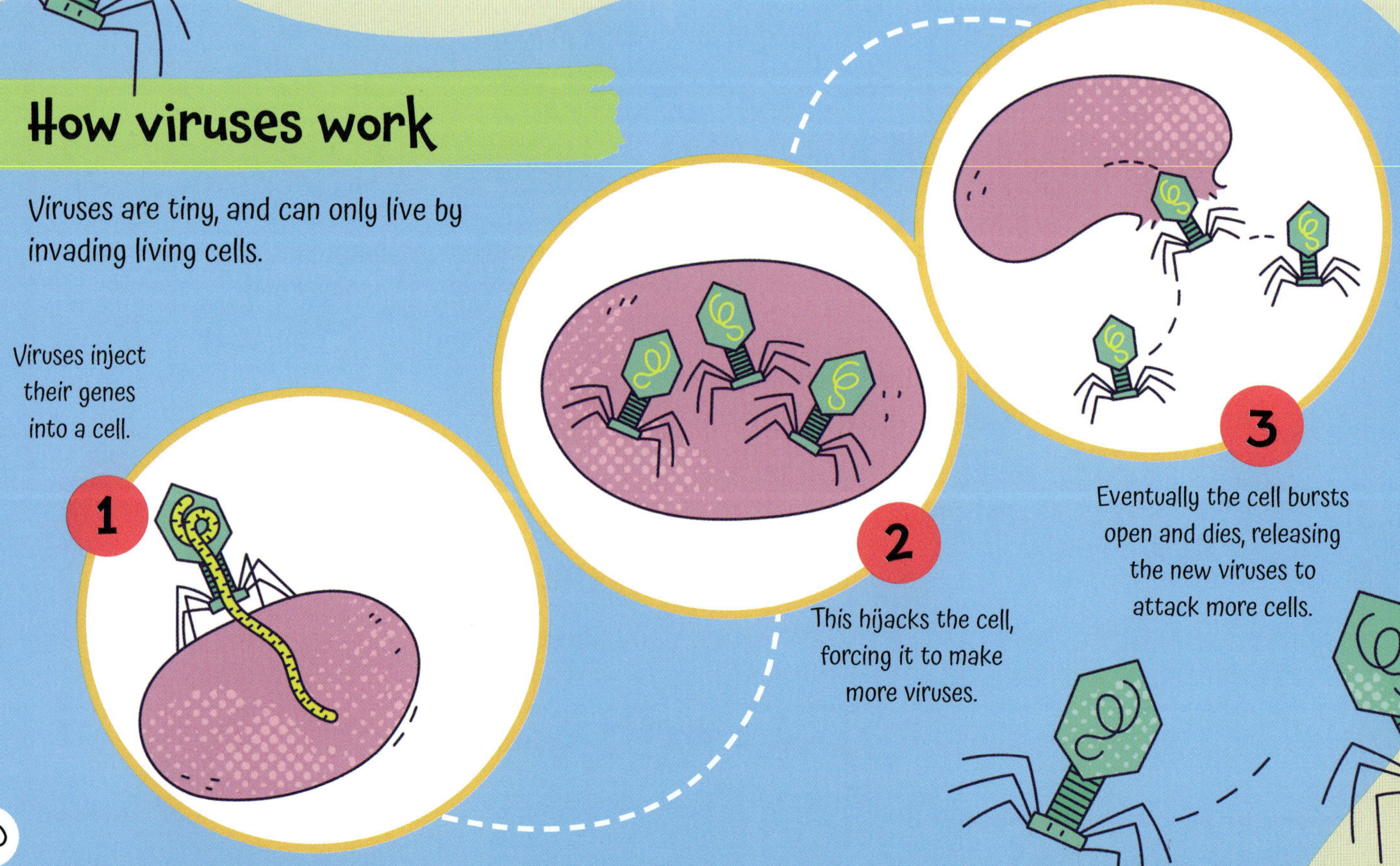

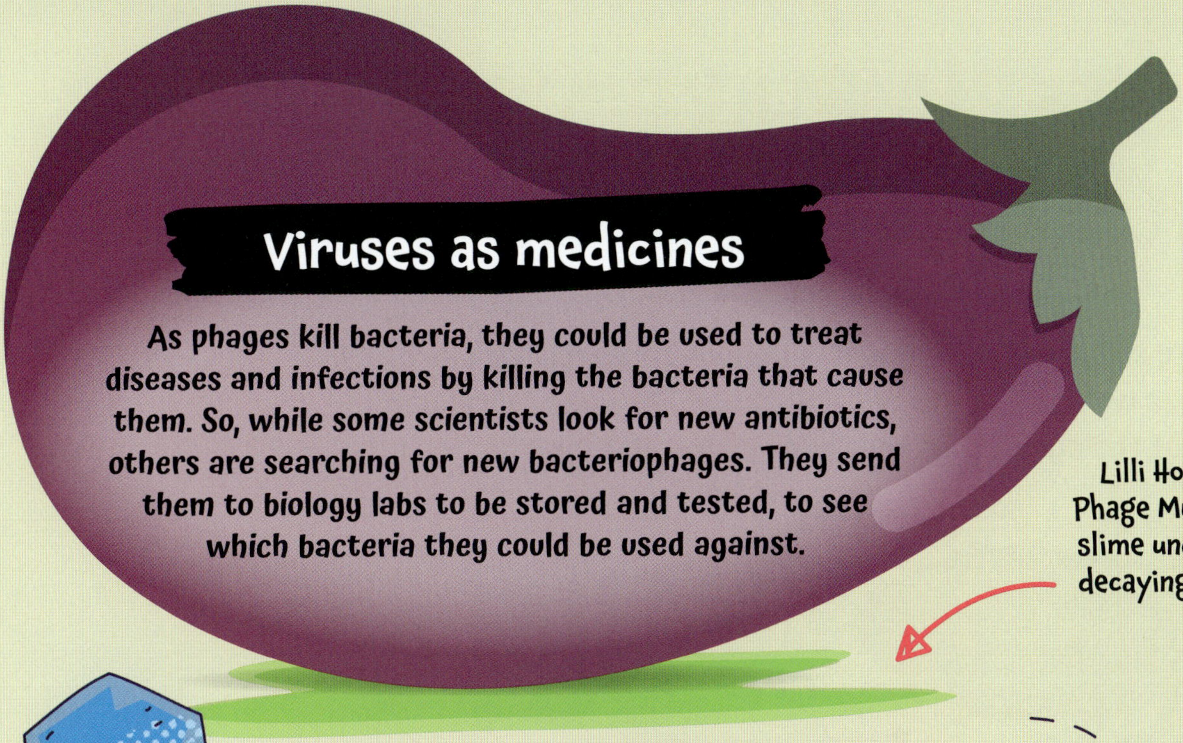

Viruses as medicines

As phages kill bacteria, they could be used to treat diseases and infections by killing the bacteria that cause them. So, while some scientists look for new antibiotics, others are searching for new bacteriophages. They send them to biology labs to be stored and tested, to see which bacteria they could be used against.

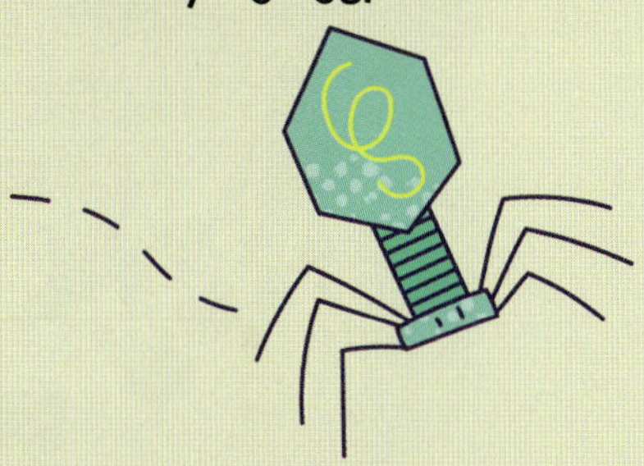

Lilli Holst found Phage Muddy in the slime underneath a decaying eggplant.

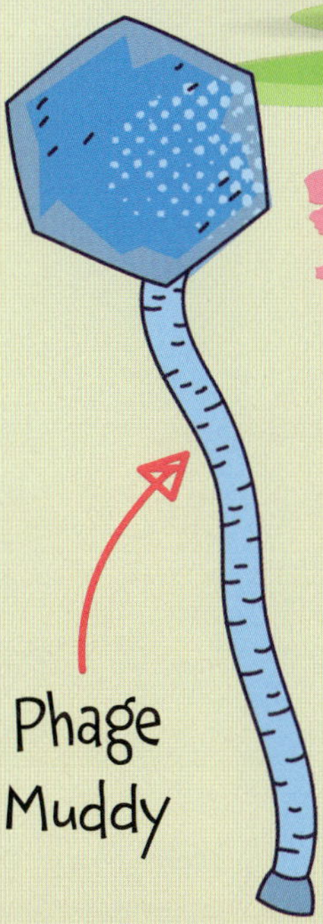

Phage Muddy

Phages to the rescue

Doctors are already experimenting with using phages to kill bacteria, known as phage therapy. In one case, a patient was seriously ill with an infection of antibiotic-resistant *Mycobacterium abscessus* bacteria after an operation.

As antibiotics couldn't help, the doctors asked the bacteriophage labs for phages that might work. Phage Muddy was the best match for the bacteria. The doctors injected it into the patient, along with two other phages, and she recovered.

In the future, phages could become a normal part of medicine.

Phage names

The person who discovers a bacteria-killing virus gets to call it whatever they like! Phage names include ...

- Zizzie
- TeddyBear
- Wheelie
- Kate
- CookieDough
- Mopey
- Giraffe
- DrSeegs
- DirtMonster

FACT FILE

NAME: PHAGE MUDDY

DISCOVERED: 2010

DISCOVERER: LILLI HOLST

SIZE: 0.4 µm LONG

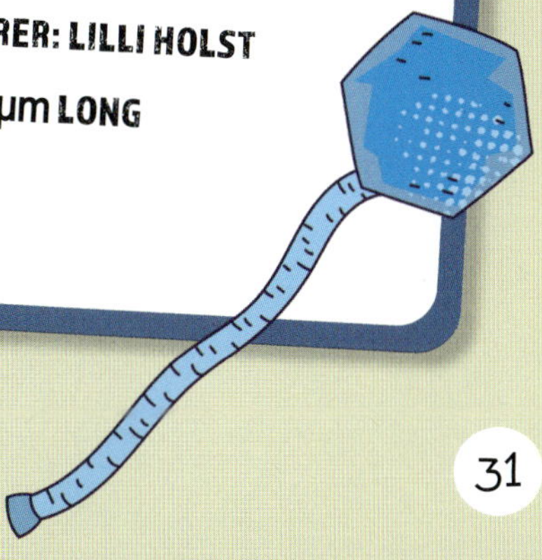

BACTERIA MAKE THE WORLD GO ROUND

The more scientists have found out about bacteria, the more they realize we couldn't live without them! They are a vital part of the cycles that keep everything else alive.

In the soil

Soil is packed with bacteria. Just one teaspoon of soil contains up to 1 billion bacteria. A whole field on a farm contains countless trillions! So what are the bacteria doing?

Fixing nitrogen

Nitrogen is a gas that makes up about 78 percent of the air. Living things like plants and animals need nitrogen to make their bodies work, but they can't take it straight out of the air. Instead, they rely on soil bacteria to turn it into chemicals they can use.

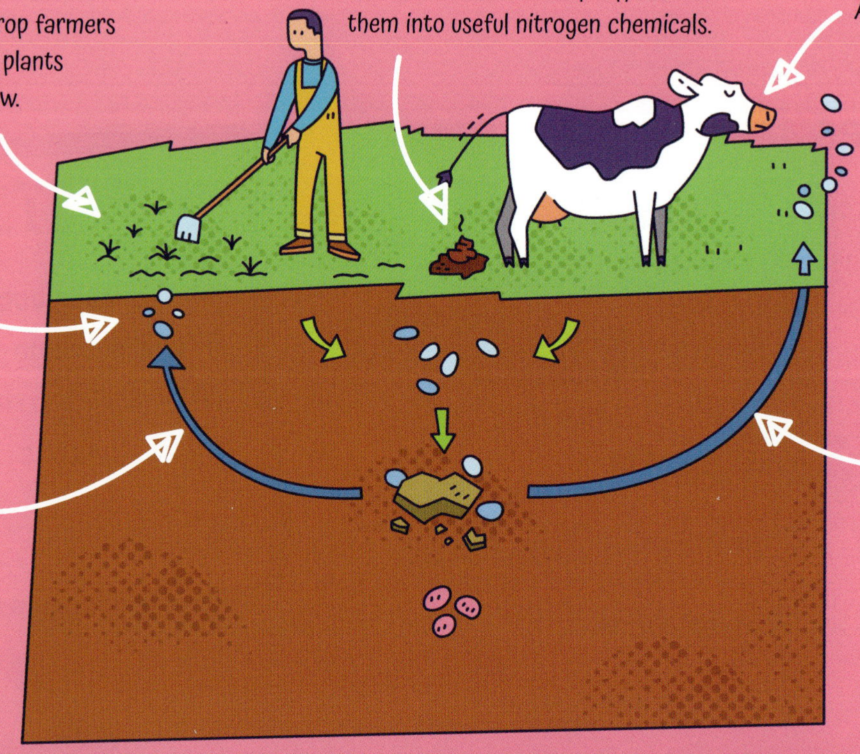

In the sea

Bacteria in the sea also take part in the nitrogen cycle, helping sea plants to grow.

They are a vital part of the ocean food chain too.

1 Ocean bacteria

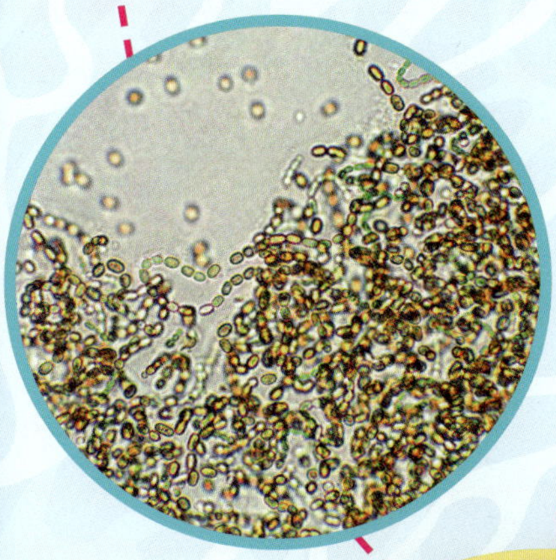

2 Bacteria provide food for plankton.

3 Plankton become food for small sea creatures, such as shrimps and sea snails.

4 They become food for fish and squid ...

5 ... which feed seabirds and seals ...

6 ... which get eaten by sharks or killer whales.

In 2020, scientists went on a two-month trip on board the Australian science ship *Investigator* to study ocean bacteria.

How many bacteria are there in the sea? Only 130 OCTILLION! That's 130,000,000,000,000,000,000,000,000,000!

BACTERIA AND FOOD

Humans began using bacteria to make food thousands of years ago – long before we even knew what bacteria were.

Fermentation

Fermentation happens when bacteria (or sometimes other microbes, such as yeasts) feed on a food, and release chemicals into it, such as acids. These change the flavor, and also kill other bacteria that would normally make it go bad so it can be kept for longer.

Fermented foods include ...

Cheese

Different types and flavors of cheese are made using different bacteria or other microbes.

Yogurt

Kefir, a fermented milk drink from western Asia

Sauerkraut, fermented cabbage popular in Germany

Coffee and chocolate – their beans are fermented to help dry them out and improve their taste.

Kimchi, Korean fermented cabbage and other vegetables

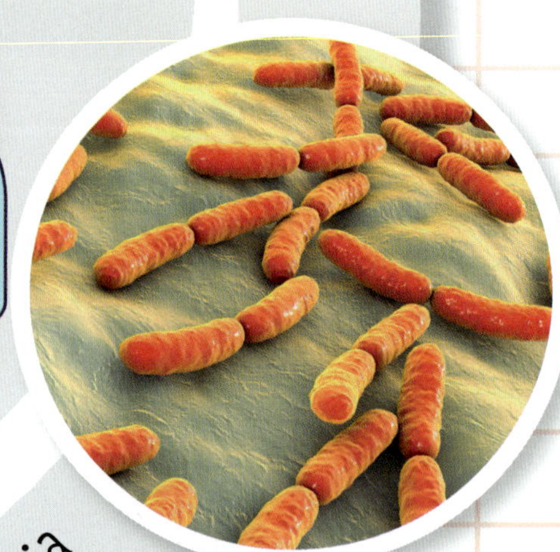

Lactobacillus plantarum bacteria are common in fermented foods.

How kimchi works

People in Korea have been making and eating kimchi for over 2,000 years, but long ago, no one knew how it worked. Since modern microscopes were invented, bacteriologists have studied kimchi to see what happens when it's made.

A cook in Korea preparing napa cabbage and other vegetables to make kimchi.

1 **First, the cabbage is covered in salt, which kills most bacteria. But natural *Lactobacillus* and a few other bacteria found on the cabbage survive, because they are salt-tolerant "halophiles" (see page 19).**

2 **The cabbage is mixed with other vegetables and spices, then stored in a jar to ferment. As the bacteria feed, they release acid, which preserves the vegetables and gives kimchi a strong, tangy taste.**

Healthy bacteria

Bacteriologists have also found that *Lactobacillus* and some other fermentation bacteria are very good for our bodies. They fight harmful germs and help us to digest food. As well as kimchi, they're found in "live" yogurt.

FERMENTATION INVENTIONS

Scientists are experimenting with fermenting bacteria that can produce other useful things too, such as biodegradable plastics.

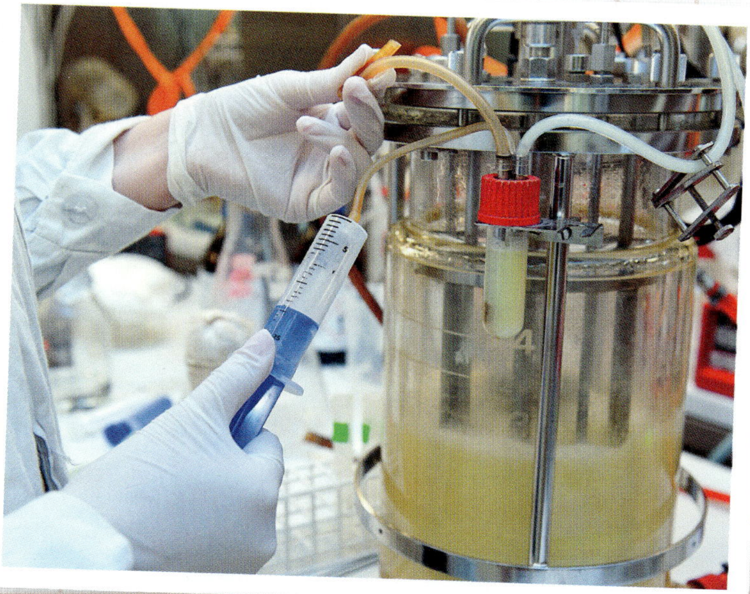

This lab fermenter is used for fermentation experiments.

LIVING WITH US

Your body is made up of over 30 trillion (30,000,000,000,000) human cells. But you are also home to roughly the same number of bacteria.

Mobile home

Humans and bacteria live in symbiosis, meaning we help each other. We give bacteria a home in our noses, mouths, on our skin, and most of all in our intestines, or guts. Some of them help us by keeping other, more dangerous bacteria away. Others eat food we can't digest (such as fiber), and release useful chemicals and vitamins.

Where bacteria live

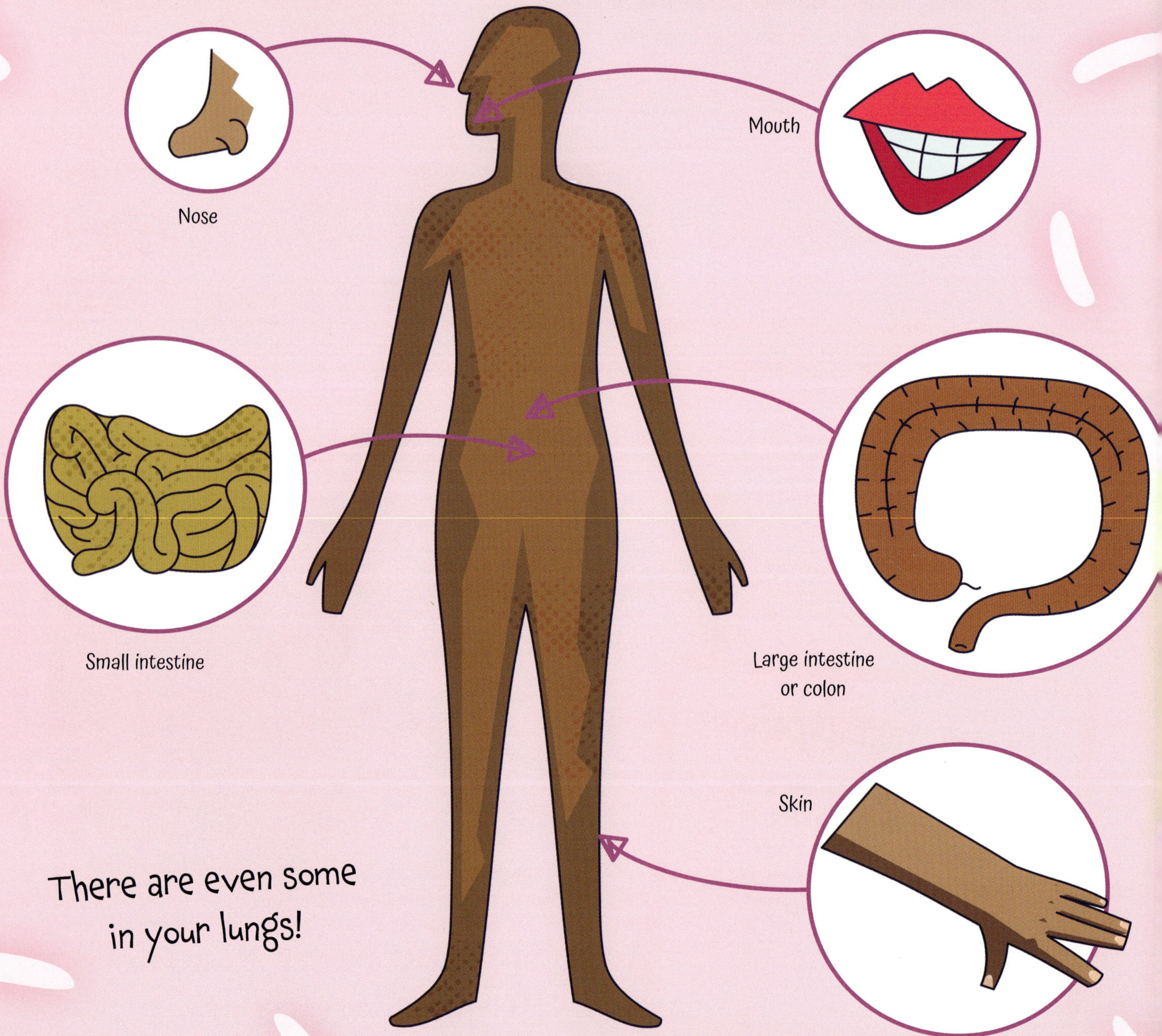

There are even some in your lungs!

Microbiome science

Bacteriologists and scientists are still finding out more about the microbes that live in us, known as the "microbiome."

Appendix discovery

The appendix, a finger-shaped tube linked to the large intestine, was once thought to be useless. But since 2007, scientists have found it keeps a store of healthy gut bacteria. If you've been ill and lost some bacteria, the appendix starts them growing again.

Poop transplants

Having lots of good gut bacteria keeps you healthy. So people who don't have enough can now have a "fecal transplant" – meaning a donation of gut bacteria from someone else's poop! It contains living bacteria that will be happy to grow in a new host.

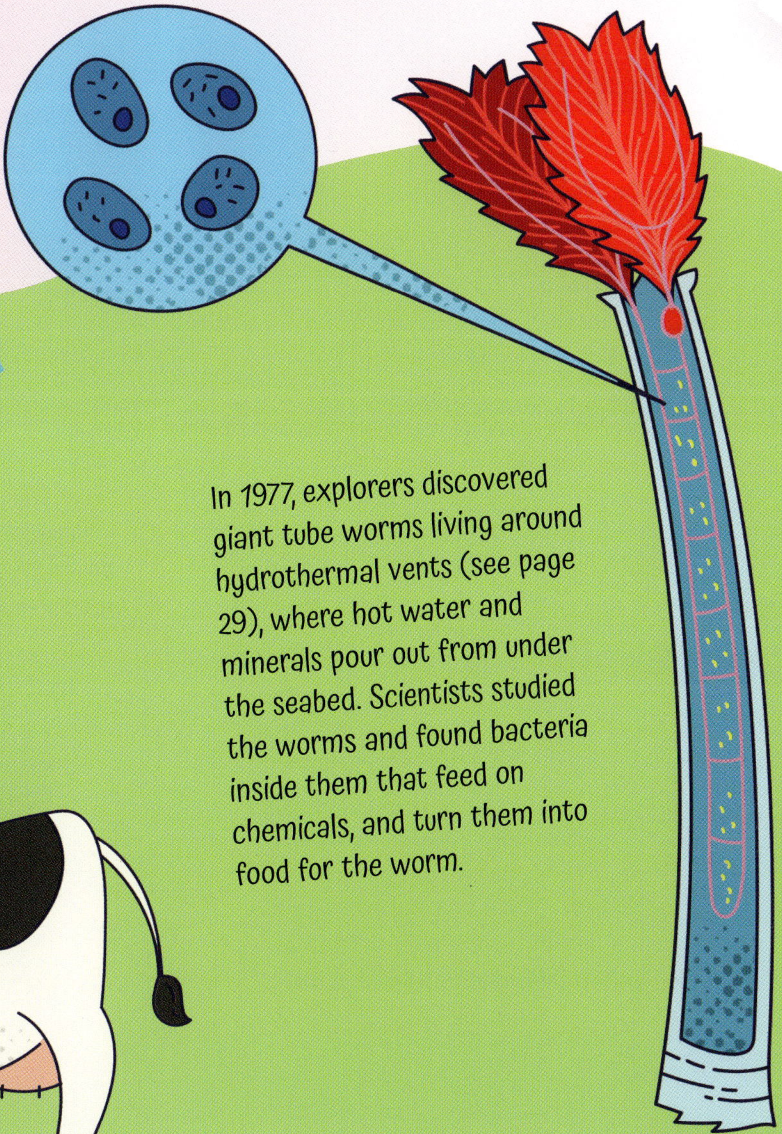

Animals and bacteria

Many other animals live in symbiosis with bacteria too.

Termites and cows have bacteria in their stomachs that help them to digest cellulose, a tough substance found in wood and grass.

In 1977, explorers discovered giant tube worms living around hydrothermal vents (see page 29), where hot water and minerals pour out from under the seabed. Scientists studied the worms and found bacteria inside them that feed on chemicals, and turn them into food for the worm.

Case Study

Bright lights at night

Meet the Hawaiian bobtail squid, a tiny, very cute squid from the Pacific Ocean. It glows with light at night, thanks to the bacteria that live inside it.

Living together

The bobtail squid lives in symbiosis with just one species of bacteria, *Vibrio fischeri*. This bacterium is bioluminescent, meaning it can light up. The bacteria live in a special light organ on the underside of the squid.

The Hawaiian bobtail squid is only about 3 inches (8 cm) long, including its tentacles.

Night light

At night, the bacteria light up, making the squid's underside glow with bluish light. This helps the squid to hide from hunters and sneak up on prey.

How does it work?

American scientist Margaret McFall-Ngai has been studying bobtail squid and their bacteria for over 30 years. She discovered how they work together.

Baby squid don't have the bacteria. They have to find them in the sea water and let them into their bodies. Once a squid has some bacteria, its light organ grows bigger.

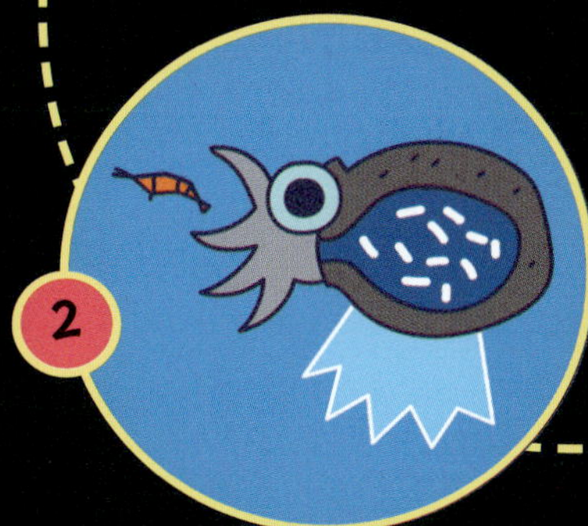

Each night, the bacteria glow as the squid goes hunting. The squid can control how strong the glow is to match the brightness of the moon.

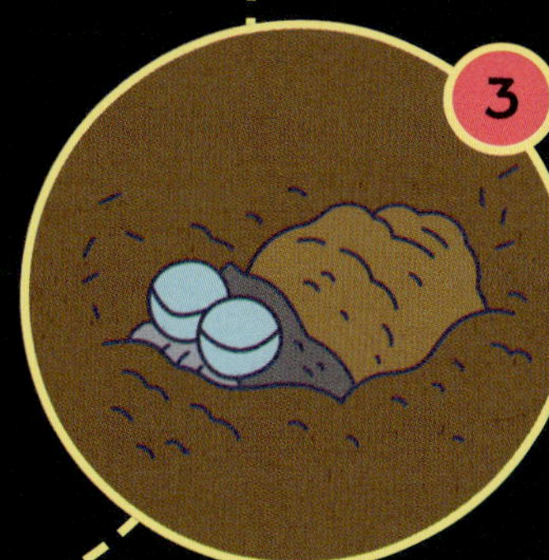

During the day, the squid burrows into the sandy seabed to sleep. It pushes most of its bacteria out of its body into the sea, where baby bobtails can find them.

As the squid sleeps, the remaining bacteria grow and multiply, feeding on food the squid makes for them. By nightfall, there are enough bacteria to make the squid light up again.

Professor McFall-Ngai collects specimens from the shallow seabed in Hawaii.

FACT FILE

NAME: *VIBRIO FISCHERI*

DISCOVERED: 1966

SHAPE: BACILLUS (ROD-SHAPED)

GRAM TYPE: GRAM-NEGATIVE

SIZE: ABOUT 2 μm LONG

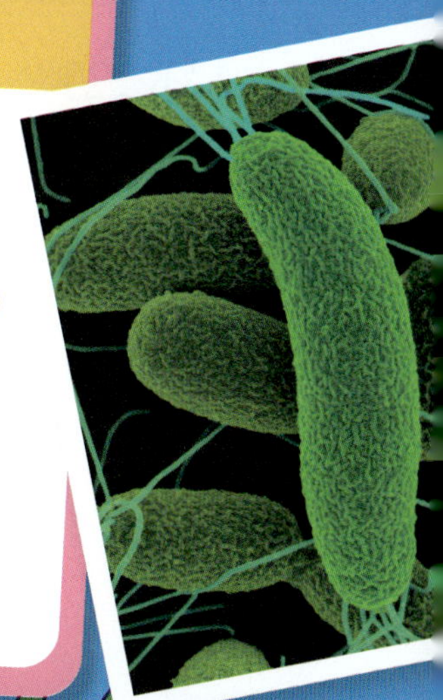

MAKING CHANGES

Bacteria can change their own DNA – and now, we can change their DNA too. Scientists do this to make bacteria do useful things for us.

American microbiologist Herbert Boyer created the first GM bacteria in the 1970s.

Changing genes

Changing the genes of living things is called genetic modification, or GM. Scientists first tried doing this in the 1970s, using *E. coli* bacteria.

Scientists take a gene from DNA from a human cell. It contains instructions for making insulin, an important body chemical.

To separate the gene, they use restriction enzymes, chemicals that cut DNA in particular places.

Here you can see how a human gene gets added to an *E. coli* bacterium:

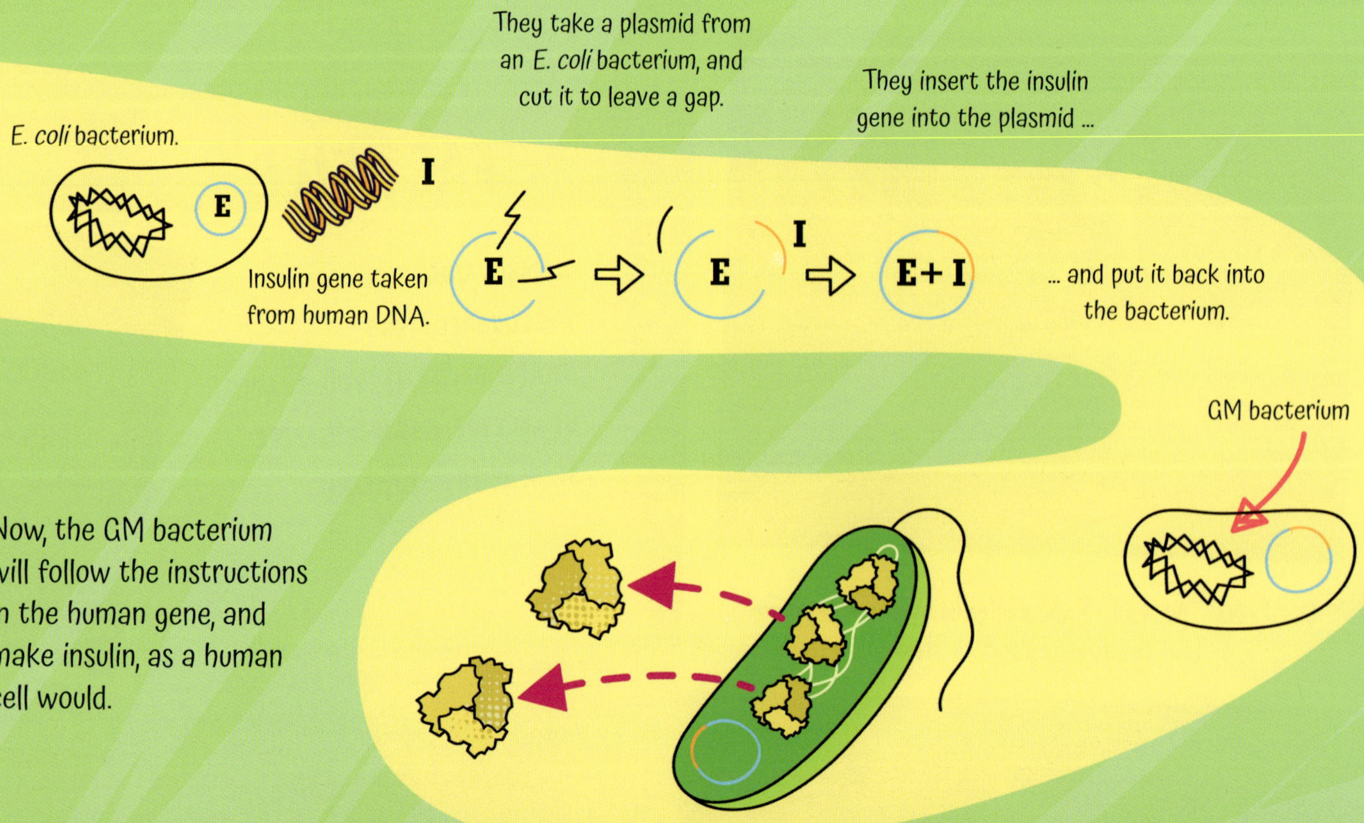

Now, the GM bacterium will follow the instructions in the human gene, and make insulin, as a human cell would.

Medicine factory

Next, the scientists let the bacterium divide and multiply, making lots more copies of itself. The bacteria are put in a big vat with plenty of food, where they make lots of insulin. It's collected, cleaned, and purified, and used as a medical treatment for people with diabetes, whose bodies can't make enough insulin.

These giant vats are full of GM bacteria making insulin.

COULD IT GO WRONG?

What if you accidentally created a killer disease bacteria instead of something useful? This is unlikely, but GM bacteria are always safety-tested and monitored to check they are not harmful.

More uses

GM bacteria are now used to make lots of other useful things too ...

- Ingredients for making cheese, fruit juice and sugar syrup

- Aspartame, a sweetener used in food and drinks

- Medicines for cancer, anaemia (lack of iron), and strokes

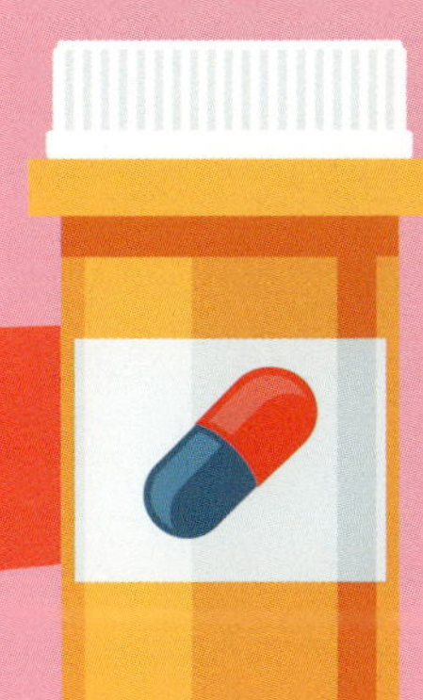

INTO THE FUTURE

What will bacteriologists of the future be doing? They're going to be busier than ever!

More to discover

Scientists think there could be millions or even billions of bacteria species waiting to be discovered. Finding and studying new bacteria could help us understand diseases better and discover new ways bacteria can help us, so it's an important job for future bacteriologists.

In 2021, a new bacteria species was found on the International Space Station, and named *Methylobacterium ajmalii* after Indian scientist Ajmal Khan. It helps plants to grow and could be used in the future to help grow crops in space.

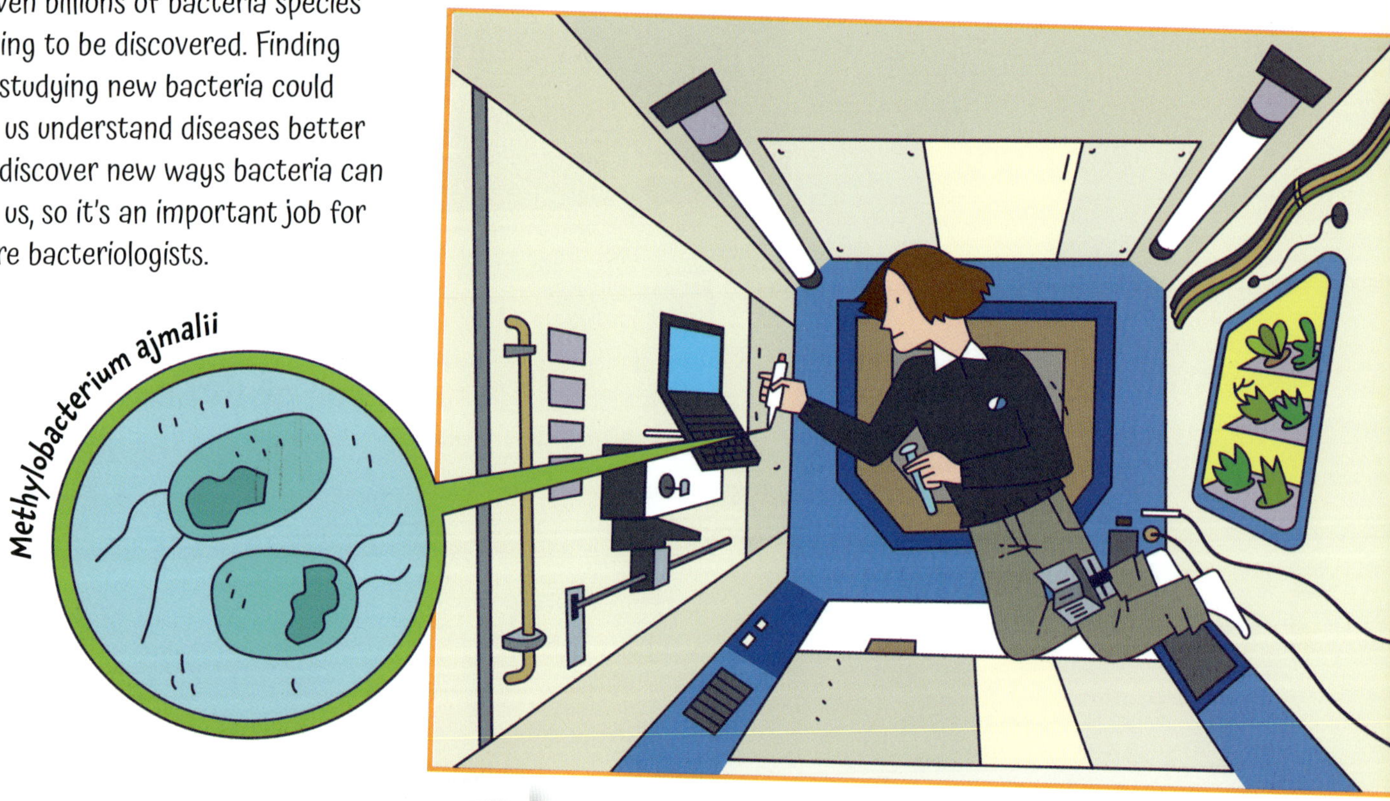

The *Perseverance* rover landed on Mars in 2021 to search for past or present life.

BACTERIA IN SPACE

If we discover aliens, they probably won't be little green humanoids or tentacle-waving blobs, but microscopic life forms, similar to bacteria. Scientists called astromicrobiologists help to search for them by looking for signs of microscopic life on other planets.

Climate change

Bacteriologists are working on how global warming is affecting bacteria – and also on how bacteria could help us to fight climate change.

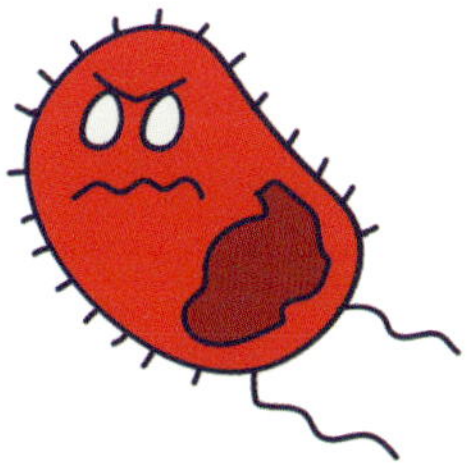

Not so good ...

- Warmer temperatures can help some disease bacteria to grow and spread faster.
- Climate change causes flooding, which can spread bacteria into clean water supplies.
- Some bacteria release carbon dioxide, adding to climate change.

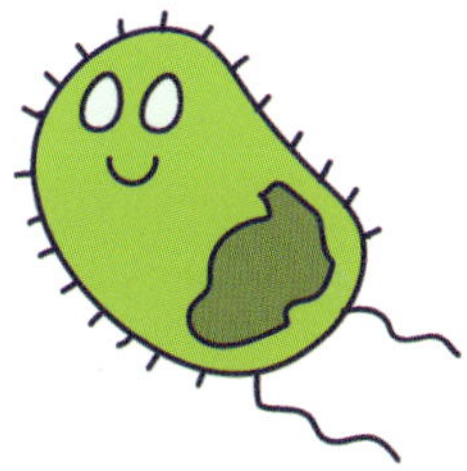

On the plus side ...

- We could find bacteria, or create GM bacteria, that help with climate change.

  They could do things like ...

  ... turning greenhouse gases into more useful substances – maybe even food.

  ... feeding on plastic waste and breaking it down into harmless chemicals.

  ... making pollution-free hydrogen fuel.

  ... making new materials for clothes, packaging, or building, that don't damage the environment.

In 2016, Japanese scientists discovered this bacterium, *Ideonella sakaiensis*, which can feed on the type of plastic used to make plastic bottles and polyester clothes.

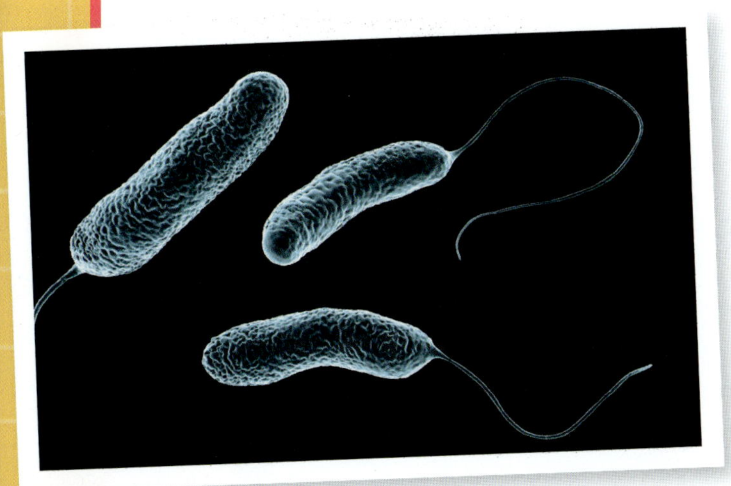

Bacteria could help to clean up plastic waste from the environment.

IS BACTERIOLOGY YOUR OLOGY?

Could you be a bacteriologist of the future? Let's hope so, because we're going to need plenty of them. But how do you become a bacteriologist?

Skills and qualities

Are you cut out to be a brilliant bacteriologist? It will definitely help if you can check off a few of these useful qualities ...

• Practical and hands-on

Bacteriology is the kind of science where you get to do lots of practical experiments, using test tubes, petri dishes, pipettes, powerful microscopes, and high-tech lab machines. If you like science experiments, you'll love it.

• Like people!

Bacteriologists don't just work with bacteria. They often work in teams, and many have jobs in universities where they teach bacteria science to students.

• Careful, clean and tidy

When you're working with bacteria, they could get anywhere. To make sure your experiments work (and you don't catch a deadly bug), you need to follow strict rules and keep everything clean and in the right place.

It IS true that Alexander Fleming (see page 27) found penicillin in a dirty petri dish that he had forgotten to wash. But normally, being messy will just mess with your results.

SUBJECTS TO STUDY

Which school subjects are the best choices for a budding bacteriologist?

Biology is the most important one, as it's the study of living things.

As with all sciences, **math** is very useful too, and so is **chemistry**.

In college, studying **microbiology**, **biology**, **biochemistry**, or **medicine** could all lead to working in bacteria science.

Bacteriology jobs

You don't even have to be a bacteriologist to work with bacteria. You could be ...

- A doctor or health expert studying bacterial diseases
- An inventor working on new ways to control or use bacteria
- A science author, journalist, or presenter, explaining bacteria to the public
- There are even artists who use bacteria to make their artwork!

GLOSSARY

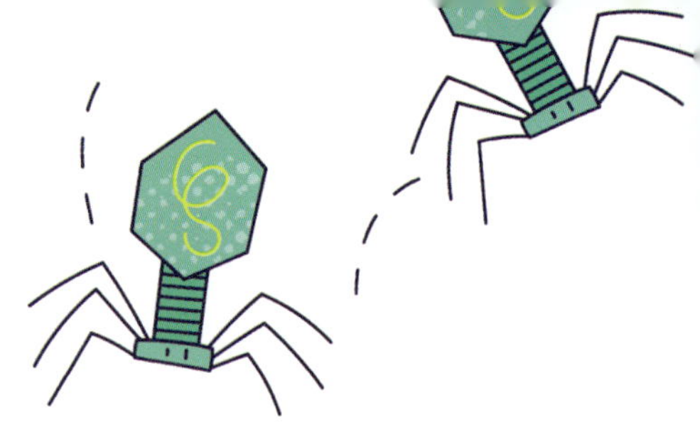

agar Jelly-like substance made using seaweed.

agar plate A petri dish containing agar mixed with other foods for bacteria to grow on.

antibiotic-resistant bacteria Bacteria that have become resistant to antibiotics and cannot be killed by them.

antibiotics Medicines that kill bacteria.

bacteria Very small, single-celled microorganisms, found in almost every habitat.

bacteriologist A scientist who studies bacteria.

bacteriology The study of bacteria.

bacteriophage A type of virus that attacks bacteria.

bases Four chemicals that form different patterns in DNA, acting as a genetic code.

binary fission The process of a bacterium splitting in half to become two new bacteria.

bioluminescence The ability of a living thing to glow with light.

cell capsule An outer layer surrounding some types of bacteria.

cells The tiny building blocks that make up living things.

cell wall A strong outer covering surrounding the cell membrane of a bacterium.

cilia Tiny hair-like parts found on the outsides of some types of cells.

climate change A long-term change in climate and weather patterns.

colon Another name for the large intestine.

colony A group of single-celled living things, such as bacteria, living together.

culture To encourage bacteria to grow and multiply in order to study them.

cytoplasm Jelly-like substance found inside most cells.

DNA (short for deoxyribonucleic acid) A chemical found in cells, used to encode instructions that make the cell work.

evolution A process of gradual change over multiple generations of living things.

extremophile A bacterium or other living thing that prefers to live in extreme conditions such as intense heat.

fermentation Allowing particular types of bacteria or other microbes to feed on food in order to change it; used to make things like yogurt and cheese.

flagellum A long whip-like or tail-like part found on some bacteria.

fungi A group of living things that includes mushrooms, molds, and yeast.

gene A sequence of bases arranged along a section of DNA, which acts as coded instructions for cells.

genetic To do with genes.

genetic modification (GM) Changing one or more of a living thing's genes to change the way it grows or lives.

genus A closely related group of species.

germs Tiny living things that can cause diseases in other living things.

GM Short for genetic modification or genetically modified.

Gram stain A test used to identify different types of bacteria by staining them with dye.

greenhouse gases Gases, such as carbon dioxide, that trap heat in the Earth's atmosphere, leading to global warming.

immune system Body system that works to keep out or kill bacteria and other germs.

infect To get into the body and start breeding and growing.

intestines Tubes inside the body that extract useful chemicals from food and collect waste.

lab Short for laboratory, a room or building where scientists do tests or experiments.

large intestine A wider, shorter part of intestine that collects waste.

microbe A microscopic living thing.

microbiology The study of microscopic living things.

microbiome A community of microbes living in or on the human body.

micrometer A tiny unit of measurement, 1,000th of a millimeter long.

mold A type of fungus that often grows on old food or in damp places.

mucus Gloopy substance made by the body, such as snot.

nitrogen An element found in the air as a gas, and also as an important part of soil and living things.

pasteurize To heat food to kill germs.

penicillin A type of antibiotic made by a mold, discovered in 1928.

petri dish A small, shallow glass or plastic dish used in labs to grow bacteria.

phage Another name for a bacteriophage.

pili Small hair-like parts that grow on the outside of some bacteria.

plankton Tiny living things that drift around in sea or pond water.

plasma membrane The inner layer of the covering of a bacterium.

plasmid A small, usually loop-shaped piece of DNA often found in bacteria, which is separate from the rest of the bacterium's DNA.

quorum sensing The way some bacteria can sense how many other bacteria are in their colony or group.

restriction enzyme A type of chemical that can cut DNA into sections.

ribosome Small part inside a bacterium or other cell, that follows instructions in the genes to make useful substances.

single-celled Having only one cell.

small intestine A longer, smaller part of the intestines that soaks up useful chemicals from food.

species The scientific name for a particular type of living thing.

strain A new form or variety of a bacterium or other microbe.

superbug A harmful strain of bacteria that has become resistant to antibiotics.

symbiosis Two or more different species living together and helping each other to survive.

thermal spring A natural spring where water heated by volcanic rock underground flows out onto Earth's surface.

tick A small, eight-legged animal related to spiders, that feeds on other animals' blood.

vaccination or vaccine A medicine that teaches the body how to fight off the germs of a particular disease.

virus A type of very small germ that can invade living cells and use them to make copies of itself. Some viruses cause diseases.

yeast A type of single-celled fungus.

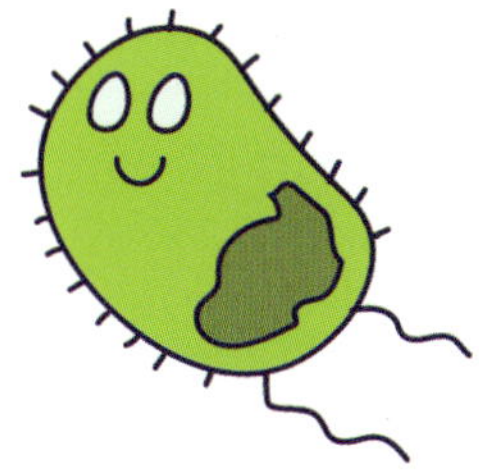

Further reading

BOOKS

Germs: Zoom in on Viruses, Bacteria, Protozoa and Much More!
By Anna Claybourne
(Gareth Stevens Publishing, 2025)

See Inside the Microscopic World
By Rosie Dickins and Peter Allen
(Usborne Publishing, 2022)

Micro Life: Miracles of the Miniature World Revealed
Foreword by Chris Packham
(Dorling Kindersley, 2022)

WEBSITES

American Museum of Natural History: Microbiology
Facts, activities, games, and quizzes about microbes, plus interviews with real-life microbiologists.
www.amnh.org/explore/ology/microbiology

Bacterial World: Museum of Natural History, University of Oxford
Online version of the Bacterial World exhibition, with lots of info, pictures, and videos.
www.oum.ox.ac.uk/bacterialworld

Note to parents and teachers: every effort has been made by the Publishers to ensure websites are suitable for children, that they are of the highest educational value, and that they contain no inappropriate or offensive material. However, because of the nature of the Internet, it is impossible to guarantee that the contents of these sites will not be altered. We strongly advise that Internet access is supervised by a responsible adult.

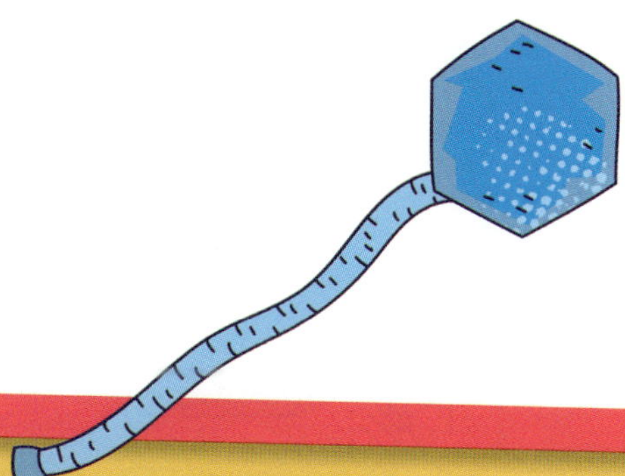

INDEX

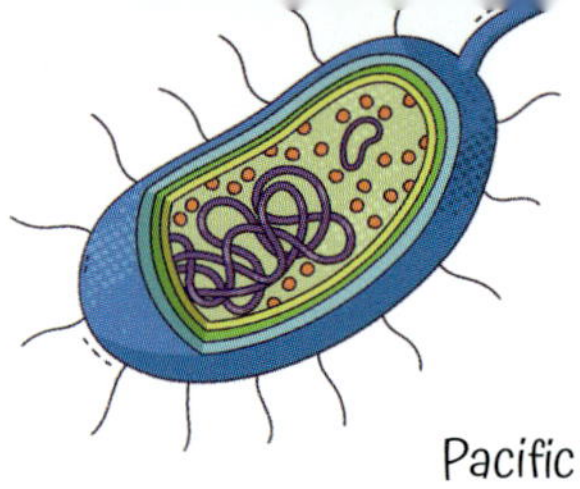

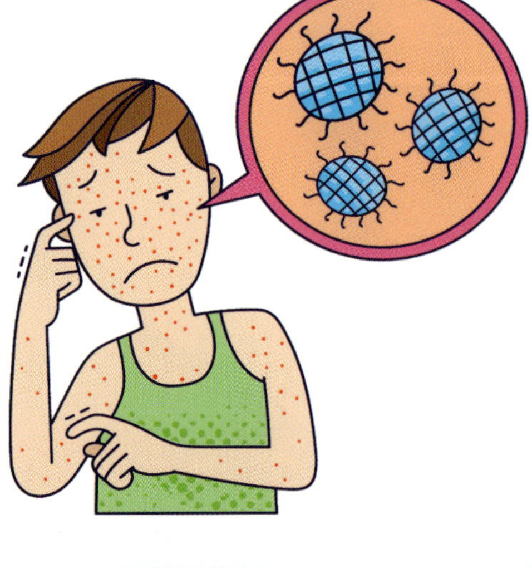